# JAMES JOYCE AND THE REVOLUTION
# OF THE WORD

# JAMES JOYCE AND THE REVOLUTION OF THE WORD

Colin MacCabe

**BOOKS**
10 East 53d St., New York 10022
(a division of Harper & Row Publishers, Inc.)

*First published 1979 by*
THE MACMILLAN PRESS LTD
*London and Basingstoke*

Published in the U.S.A. 1979 by
HARPER & ROW PUBLISHERS, INC.
BARNES & NOBLE IMPORT DIVISION

Printed in Great Britain

**Library of Congress Cataloging in Publication Data**

MacCabe, Colin.
  James Joyce and the revolution of the word.
  Bibliography: p.
  Includes index.
  1. Joyce, James, 1882–1941—Criticism and
  interpretation. I. Title.
  PR6019.09Z718 1979        823′.9′12        79–10830
  ISBN 0–06–494438–7

Et tout va recommencer au-delà de la réunification, du plein, de la complétude, du tout, dans cet autre battement de l'un et du multiple qui ne peut s'écrire que *de nouveau*. Et c'est cette saturation des variétés polymorphiques, polyphoniques, polygraphiques, polyglottiques, de la sexualité; cette *déprise* de la sexualité; cette ironisation ravageante de vos désirs les plus viscéraux, répétés, qui vous laissent, avouez-le, embarrassés devant Joyce. Freud, Joyce: une autre ère pour l'humanité.*

*Philippe Sollers*

* And everything will begin again beyond the reunification, the fullness, the completeness, in that other beating rhythm of the one and the multiple which can only be written *anew*. It is this saturation of the polymorphic, polyphonic, polygraphic, polyglottic, varieties of sexuality, this *unsetting* of sexuality, this devastating ironicalisation of your most visceral, repeated, desires which leaves you – admit it – troubled when faced with Joyce. Freud, Joyce: another era for manwomankind.

For Myles, Ruth and John

# Contents

# Acknowledgements

The author and publishers wish to thank the following who have kindly given permission for the use of copyright material.

The Bodley Head and Random House Inc., for the extracts from *Ulysses*, U.S. copyright 1914, 1918 by Margaret Caroline Anderson and renewed 1942, 1946 by Nora Joseph Joyce, and Jonathan Cape Ltd on behalf of the Executors of the James Joyce Estate and The Viking Press Inc., for the extracts from *Dubliners*, originally published in 1916 in the U.S. by B. W. Huebsch Inc., copyright © 1967 by the Estate of James Joyce, and the extracts from *A Portrait of the Artist as a Young Man*, U.S. copyright © 1916 by B. W. Huebsch Inc., 1944 by Nora Joyce, copyright © 1964 by the Estate of James Joyce. We also thank Jonathan Cape Ltd on behalf of the Executors of the James Joyce Estate and The Society of Authors as literary representatives for the extracts from *Stephen Hero*.

Faber and Faber Ltd and The Viking Press Inc., for the extracts from *The Critical Writings of James Joyce* edited by Ellsworth Mason and Richard Ellmann, U.S. copyright © 1959 by Harriet Weaver and F. Lionel Monro, as administrators of the Estate of James Joyce, and the extracts from *Letters of James Joyce* edited by Richard Ellmann, U.S. copyright © 1966 by F. Lionel Monro as administrator of the Estate of James Joyce. The Society of Authors as the literary representatives of the Estate of James Joyce and The Viking Press Inc., for the extracts from *Finnegans Wake*, U.S. copyright © 1939 by James Joyce, © 1967 by George Joyce and Lucia Joyce, and for the poem 'Dooleysprudence' from *The Critical Writings of James Joyce*.

# Preface

This work is a version of a doctoral thesis and no doubt it bears the scars of its genesis.

In its elaboration I have drawn on a multitude of friends and enemies. I hope most of my borrowings are acknowledged within the text but it is doubtful if I could make clear the extent of my indebtedness to two friends, Stephen Heath and Ben Lloyd. In addition I should personally thank the following for their contribution: Paul Abbott, David Bleiman, Ben Brewster, Jocelyn Cornwell, Jonathan Culler, Terry Counihan, Charles Larmore, Stuart MacIntyre, Richard Nice, Pat Parrinder, Jean-Michel Rabaté, Jacqueline Rose and Tony Tanner.

It might have been more appropriate to have talked of the various institutions in which discussion took place rather than the individual with whom I communicated. Three institutions demand such identification: the Ecole Normale Supérieure, Paris, where a seminar on *Finnegans Wake* solved some initial theoretical problems, Emmanuel College, Cambridge, which awarded me a Research Fellowship that enabled me to complete this work, and *Screen* magazine where, as a member of the editorial board, I was frequently reminded of the inadequacy of a purely literary discourse.

There remains the most important of institutions: the family. It is from my own that I have learnt the configurations of exile, guilt and mania which compose Irish Catholicism. Without such lessons I would not have been able to read Joyce. I undertook this thesis for many reasons but its happiest result, which could perhaps have been realised in other and better ways, is that I realise that my family is the best I could possibly have.

*Cambridge*
*6 January 1978*                                     COLIN MACCABE

# Abbreviations

The primary texts used in this work are all British editions of Joyce's work. The following abbreviations are adopted:

*Dubliners*, London, 1967 (D followed by the page number)

*Stephen Hero*, London, 1969 (SH followed by the page number)

*A Portrait of the Artist as a Young Man*, London, 1968 (P followed by the page number)

*The Critical Writings of James Joyce*, London, 1959 (CW followed by the page number)

*Ulysses*, London, 1960 (page numbers without any preceding symbol)

*Finnegans Wake*, London, 1975 (page and line numbers without any preceding symbol)

Full bibliographical details can be found at the end of the text.

# 1

# Theoretical Preliminaries

The title *James Joyce and the Revolution of the Word* presupposes a
relation between politics and language, and, further, that this
relation is of relevance to the works of James Joyce.[1] It is the
purpose of this work to demonstrate the correctness of these
presuppositions. The politics of Joyce's texts will not become
the explicit focus of concern until the last two chapters of the
book. This direct confrontation will, however, follow an analysis of Joyce's use of language which is, itself, political. For
Joyce's writing produces a change in the relations between
reader and text, a change which has profound revolutionary
implications. It is an understanding of both the politics of reading and the reading of politics which will allow an evaluation of
the revolutionary potential and the actual political ineffectiveness of Joyce's work.

In understanding Joyce's texts politically there will be a con-

[1] The title also has a history. In 1929 Eugene Jolas published a manifesto
entitled 'The Revolution of the Word' in *transition*, the journal which was pub-
lishing *Work in Progress*. This manifesto appropriated the political for the aesthetic and located historic change in the choice of language made by
individual writers. F.R. Leavis, in a famous *Scrutiny* review, 'James Joyce and
the Revolution of the Word', argued for the incorrectness of Jolas's voluntaristic analysis but kept the argument centred on the individual writer
(Leavis 1933a). To give sense to the phrase it is crucial to shift attention from
individual writers to conflicting practices of writing. Such a shift allows a consideration of sexuality as a necessary third term in the relations between politics and language. 'The Revolution of the Word Made Flesh' would, in its
multiple ambiguity, capture the three-term relation that this work will investigate.

1

stant emphasis that they must be read as practices of writing. This emphasis is designed to draw attention to the fact that Joyce's writing is concerned with the material effects of language and with the possibilities of transformation. The traditional Marxist definition of a practice is a transformation of material through work, and in reading Joyce we are continually forced to work on our discourses in an unceasing transformation of both them and ourselves. The difficulty of reading Joyce is a difficulty in our notion of reading. Reading for us is passive consumption; with Joyce it becomes an active metamorphosis, a constant displacement in language.

This metamorphosis and displacement presents literary criticism with its own impossibility. Interpretation as the search for meaning must cease when both meaning and interpreter become functions of the traverse of the material of language. In its place we might begin the study of the positions offered to the subject within language and of how literature confirms and subverts those possibilities. Such a study might eventually offer a history of the mutations of these positions and the relation of those mutations to the political, economic and ideological history in which they take place. It should be stressed that this discipline would have nothing to do with a sociology of literature in which literature is read as a representation of society but would concern itself with the changing relation of the body to language (more exactly, of the body in language) through time. *Finnegans Wake* would be a primer for this new discipline.

Before undertaking the analysis of Joyce's practices of writing, it is necessary to consider briefly the inadequacies of the discourse of literary criticism. It would be comforting to pretend, as most literary critics do, that literary criticism is unimportant, a transient epiphenomenon which can be ignored in favour of the original literary text. It is true that particular works of literary criticism appear and disappear with startling rapidity and no obvious effectivity. But the discourses and institutions of literary criticism, which support and make possible individual critical works, permit and condition our reading. To pretend that we can go direct to the text is to take literary criticism at its word and believe that the text is a simple and definable object. But every text is already articulated with other texts which determine its possible meaning and no text can escape the discourses of literary criticism in which it is referred to, named and identified.

The theoretical inadequacy of literary criticism, demonstrable for any work, is compounded by its practical failure with Joyce. To write about Joyce is to write about an author who is universally acknowledged as great but who is little read except by those who make his work their major preoccupation. This charge is doubly damning if one considers, as I do, that he is the major writer in English since Shakespeare. If many have read *A Portrait of the Artist as a Young Man*, few have read *Ulysses* with the necessary attention and fewer still have done more than open *Finnegans Wake*. Literary criticism – and there is no shortage of books devoted to Joyce – preserves him as unread. In part this lack of readers relates to features of the text but the situation has been aggravated by the persistent refusal of commentators to engage with the radical novelty of Joyce's work. Instead Joyce's texts are transformed into complicated crossword puzzles whose solution is the banal liberal humanism of the critic. The reason for the failure of the critics to give an account of Joyce's texts is not some congenital inability on their part but that literary criticism itself cannot cope with Joyce's texts because those texts refuse to reproduce the relation between reader and text on which literary criticism is predicated. The literary critic labours under the same delusion as Professor Jones in *Finnegans Wake*. He is unable to decipher the letter because he mistakes its very constitution; his error is not that he cannot find the right interpretation but that he tries to interpret at all. The aim of this work is not to provide the meaning of Joyce's work but to allow it to be read. Hence, problems concerning the discourse of literary criticism (more colloquially, the habits of reading that have developed over the last 150 years) will be a constant focus of attention.

Central to the discourse of literary criticism is the philosophical category of the subject. This category, under a variety of names (of which 'author' is the most common), is indispensable to the very activity of literary criticism. Traditionally the function of the category was to provide a unity for the field of experience such that one could give an account of judgement between possibilities within that experience. The subject provided both the limit and the unity of experience. In constituting its own limits it gave itself a position of dominance from which to judge items within the field of experience. But in providing this unity and homogeneity it also provided something else: it allowed for the possibility of a representational theory of language.

It is only given the essential homogeneity of experience and a position from which the elements within it can be judged that it is possible to talk of a representational theory of language. If experience is heterogeneous then there can be no simple one-to-one relation between it and language, and even if it is homogeneous there can be no possibility of its representation in language unless there is a position from which word can be aligned against thing. Literary criticism depends on a theory of the subject in order to carry out its task of interpretation. Interpretation is the search for meaning and meaning is dependent on a divorce between language and the world which is both made possible and guaranteed by the subject.

Joyce's texts, however, refuse the subject any dominant position from which language could be tallied with experience. *Ulysses* and *Finnegans Wake* are concerned not with representing experience through language but with experiencing language through a destruction of representation. Instead of constructing a meaning, Joyce's texts concern themselves with the position of the subject in language. If the literary critic is interested in meaning, Joyce's texts are concerned with the various positions from which meaning becomes possible. In order to grasp the activities of Joyce's texts it becomes necessary to understand the construction of the position of the subject and what is always buried in that construction. Joyce's texts disrupt the normal position assigned to a reader in a text and thus alter the reader's relation to his or her discourses. This disruption is not merely a formal matter but also determines Joyce's concerns at the level of content.

In an attempt to understand how formal and substantial elements intertwine to produce *Ulysses* and *Finnegans Wake*, emphasis will be placed on certain psycho-analytic concepts. In order to avoid independent justification for each concept, I want to consider why these concepts figure in an analysis of Joyce and, at the same time, rebut *a priori* objections that could be raised against their use. Psycho-analysis is the name for both a theory and a practice. The practice has a limited and specific definition but the theory can be held to have relevance in our attempts to understand any signifying practice.

Anna O. characterised the treatment that Breuer created with her, and which Freud was to develop, as the 'talking cure' and if we think of the techniques of analysis (the attention to slips, free associations, jokes, dreams) we can best understand them as an elaborate work on language. The silence of the analyst and his or her refusal to enter into normal inter-subjective relations are what allows the patient in the analytic situation to reorient him or herself in language. The patient constantly hears his or her own discourse return across the silence of the analyst with a message different from that which was first entrusted to it. And it is this reorientation that allows repressed desire to find expression. Within this perspective it is possible to understand that the unconscious is not some bestial nature that has suffered a necessary, if inadequate, censorship but the inevitable result of the entry of the body into language.

The formulation of the conditions of existence of the unconscious in terms of language is associated with the Ecole Freudienne de Paris and its founder, Jacques Lacan. Lacan's work constitutes an effort to prevent psycho-analysis falling back into biologism (a theory of the empirically given body) or psychologism (a theory of the mind as authentically experienced) and to redirect attention to language as the primary material of the psycho-analytic method. To understand the force of his theories it is only necessary to consider Freud's own contradictory explanations of the existence of the unconscious. The better known version runs as follows: what is unconscious is unconscious because it involves a renunciation so terrible that the very fact of renunciation must be repressed (the little boy comes to realise that he cannot marry his mother; such a realisation is so painful that he represses the original wish and its frustration). The problem with this account is that it relies on the notion of consciousness as primary and makes the unconscious the product of a secondary and derivative *decision*. The conditions of the existence of the unconscious are grounded in a psychological theory of the 'unbearable' but there is no real weight to this 'unbearableness', there is no logical reason why the outcome could not be different. Freud's alternative suggestion is equally open to objection. Freud argued in early papers that the production of the unconscious is an effect of the child's relation to sensuous reality. Whereas, in a first moment, it cannot distinguish between reality and an hallucination which is the product of a wish, in a second, under the pressure of physical distress (the hallucinated breast does not satisfy hunger), the subject sets up defences against being misled by perception and relegates hallucinations to the unconscious. This account also depends on a conscious agency prior to the unconscious, and neither account explains why the linguistic relation holding between the analyst and the person being analysed (the analysand) can produce any privileged access to the unconscious.

Lacan argues that the unconscious is a necessary consequence of the fact that the conditions of the possibility of language are both present and absent in any moment of speech. Necessarily present as the differences that constitute the existence of meaning, the system of language is necessarily absent from that meaning (that moment of consciousness). For Lacan, it is this play between presence and absence, which is essential to the functioning of language, that constitutes us as desiring beings. Language introduces us to an existence which can never be satisfied, for, as a condition of our speech, something is always missing. And this missing thing is not an unimportant theoretical postulate but the necessarily recurrent question of our being. The process of loss which enables us to gain language produces for us a place and an identity (a name and its substitution rules) within language, but this place is produced by the necessary absence of the differences that constitute it. It is these repressed differences which make themselves heard in verbal slips where language once again reduces to the material from which it has been fashioned. The silence of the analyst allows those differences to become significant whereas in normal conversation we hurry on, embarrassed or irritated by these evidences of a lack of control. The unconscious is the result of the fact that, as we speak, what we say always escapes us – that as I (the ego) say one thing, it (the id) says something else.

Generally the use of psycho-analysis within literary criticism has remained caught within literary criticism's model of the relation of the subject to language (indeed Freud's own excursions into literary criticism often do not escape these strictures). The text is theorised as the representation of certain psychic conflicts and various elements within the text are read off in relation to the author's psyche. Psycho-analytic accounts of this kind simply replace the conscious author, matching word against world, with an unconscious one who bears the same relation to the texts. Lacan's theories suggest that it is impossible to use this framework to explain a text's functioning. Instead of understanding the text as the representation of an epistemologically distinct area (be it conscious or unconscious experience), we must conceive it as the articulation of the possibilities of experience, these possibilities being another name for the limits of our language. Psycho-analysis suggests that it is not a question of the patient's language representing (or misrepresenting) experience but rather that what I can experience is dependent on what positions the 'I' can take up in language. The inability of a patient to utter a repressed desire is not a question of vocabulary (the individual words will be there) but of discourse (the regularities of lexical combinations within both the sentence and larger units of distribution). The divorce between language and experience, on which the discourses of literary criticism depend, seems implausible in the light of the discoveries of Freud. Psycho-analysis does not understand the patient's language as representing his or her experience but investigates the position allowed to the subject within his or her discourses. The process of the cure is the process by which new discourses open up fresh positions. If one accepts these arguments then one could maintain that psycho-analytic categories will be necessary for a study of literature devoted to the investigation of the variable position of the speaking subject in discourse. Literary criticism might be understood as constructing a typology of texts in terms of the positions they offer to the reader.

Such a use of psycho-analysis, while avoiding the mistakes of traditional literary criticism, lays itself open to two further reproaches. Given that psycho-analysis has been developed within an analytic situation which depends on a certain linguistic order (that of analyst and analysand), how can one use its concepts to investigate the very different linguistic order that obtains between reader and text? Further, how can one use psycho-analysis outside the context of symptom and cure?

The first objection would hold that psycho-analytic theory is limited to the field of psycho-analytic practice. Lacan's theories would indicate that Freud's insight into language is of a far greater generality. The general and radical nature of Freud's investigation is captured by Lacan in his re-formulation of the Cartesian *cogito*. The *cogito* provides the justification for the primacy of the subject. 'I think therefore I am' situates the 'I' in simple evidence to itself and provides a moment of pure presence which can found the enterprise of judging world against word. Lacan suggests that the Freudian cogito would run: 'I think where I am not and I am where I do not think.' This formulation spells out the fundamental misunderstanding that is involved in any successful use of language. The processes of articulation which produce a position for the speaking subject are ignored, as we speak, from the very position that they have produced. The unconscious is that effect of language which escapes the conscious subject in the distance between the act of enunciation (in which the subject passes from signifier to signifier) and what is enounced (in which the subject finds him or herself in place as, for example, the pronoun 'I'). Psycho-analysis enables us to understand the subject as fundamentally divided and this division is a feature of any use of language; the analytic situation's specificity resides in the fact that it is able to bring this division to the analysand's attention in a concentrated and focused way.

The second objection, to the effect that any use of psycho-analytical categories in the analysis of literature will reduce the text to a symptom, rests on a profound misunderstanding of the role of the symptom in psycho-analytic thought. To achieve such a reduction it is necessary to understand psycho-analysis as a finished science of human behaviour which treats all behaviour as homogeneous and as symptom (that is to say expression/representation) of a definitive and inalterable construction of the subject. In other words, certain conflicts in the life of the early child determine in later life a set of symptoms amongst which one can count any literary or artistic work. This position, which *is* reductive and which Freud's own extremely problematic efforts at cultural criticism often seem to adopt, is in radical contradiction with those elements of Freudian thought which refuse any positivist notion of identity as constant through time in favour of a conception of the subject as the product of a constant re-articulation in the present. Freud used the concept of *deferred action* to avoid conferring an absolute identity on the child's life, arguing instead that a new event can produce totally new configurations in the past life of the child and endow a past event with totally new significance. The most obvious example of the working of deferred action is the male child's perception of the threat of castration. There is no need for an actual threat to be uttered by the parents. It is the realisation of the possibility of being without a penis (the realisation, that is, of sexual difference) which retroactively transforms earlier statements or events into a threat of forcible loss.

If it is impossible to fix conflicts in the past independently of their articulation in the present then it is impossible to hold apart conflict and symptom; the two are inextricably linked. Indeed this is what was at stake in the very founding moment of psycho-analysis when Freud realised that his patients' stories of infantile sexual trauma were not a reference to a real past event but were fantasies which articulated the conflict in the present. The introduction of the concept of fantasy not only collapses the boundary between conflict and symptom but also the distinction between symptom and literature. The removal of this distinction does not, however, reduce one to the other but redefines both.

The centrality of art, and particularly literature, to the very constitution of the symptom is particularly evident in those clusters of fantasies to which Freud gave the generic name 'family romance'. These fantasies, typical in children, furnish the child with an imaginary and more satisfactory family, the exact explanation of the relation between the real and imaginary family depending on the state of the child's sexual knowledge. While very young the child may treat its real parents as foster-parents acting for some couple of higher social standing, later it may be necessary to admit the mother as invariable but invent a different father! These fantasies often become conscious again in paranoia and indicate a failure of the subject to achieve a satisfactory rupture with the real family. These stories, which relate very obviously to the dominant forms of nineteenth-century fiction, indicate (what is anyway evident in any case history) that art is always inscribed in the symptom, in the conflicts, in the very fabric of neurosis. The way we locate ourselves in the Oedipal drama, in that constitutive entrance to the world of language and sexual difference is not independent of artistic forms. Problems of narration and of the interplay between narrative and discourse (an interplay on which Joyce's texts constantly insist) are fundamental in the construction of an identity.

The abandonment of positivist notions of identity and an acceptance of the reality of fantasy transform the relation of psycho-analysis and literature from the reductive model in which it has too often been defined. While psycho-analysis understands itself as a science of human behaviour, literature can be treated as a form of that behaviour and thus as an object of study. If psycho-analysis, however, considers itself as the science of the construction of the subject in language then we can pose its relation to literature not as that of science to object but as that of theory to practice. It could be argued that, in its elaboration, the theory of psycho-analysis has been as dependent on literature as on the analytic situation. Freud never tired of saying that he was only discovering what artists had discovered before him, but more important than this explicit claim is the functioning of literary quotation and reference within Freud's discourse. The nature of this functioning and its effectivity within the concepts of psycho-analysis would involve a separate study but its reality is attested to in the most famous concept of psycho-analysis, the Oedipus complex, which takes its descriptive features from a literary text: Sophocles' *Oedipus the King*.

In this context it can be taken as significant that Lacan's own elaboration of Freud involves a constant and serious attention to literature, an attention which is often absent in contemporary psycho-analytic thought. Most famously, Lacan prefaced the publication of his collected writings in 1966 with his seminar on the Edgar Allen Poe short story 'The Purloined Letter'. More directly to our purpose, the last five years have witnessed an ever increasing reference to Joyce in Lacan's work. When *Le Séminaire* XI (a transcription of lectures delivered in 1963–64) was published, Lacan included a postscript written in January 1973, in which he reflected on the fate of his earlier written work. The *Ecrits*, Lacan claimed, had been sold but had not been read, nor was this surprising as they had been written not to be read. One can gloss this negative claim as a description of a practice of writing which displaces reading as a passive consumption of a signified (meaning) and transforms it into an active organisation of signifiers (material images). This notion of reading as an active appropriation of the material of language is common both to the practice of psycho-analysis and Joyce's texts. Lacan makes this connection clear when he refers to Joyce:

> . . . après tout l'écrit comme pas-à-lire, c'est Joyce qui l'introduit, je ferais mieux de dire: l'intraduit, car à faire du mot traite au-delà des langues, il ne se traduit qu'à peine, d'être partout également peu à lire. ( . . . after all the written as the not-to-be-read is introduced by Joyce. I'd do better to say intraduced (both introduced and not translated), because to deal with the word is to negotiate beyond languages, Joyce hardly translates himself at all, so that he is equally little-to-be-read everywhere.) (Lacan 1973a, p. 252)

If, however, psycho-analysis as theory has always been dependent on those practices of writing that we know as literature as well as those practices of speech that we know as psychoanalysis, it has never acknowledged this dependence nor drawn the necessary conclusions. If we are to use psycho-analytic concepts in the analysis of literature then it will not be to study the work as the product of the life, for this would presume a divorce between symptom and conflict which we have seen to be impossible. Psycho-analysis denies to a life that independence which could allow it to function as origin for the work. What one can attempt to study is how the work relates to the forms in which it is written and how those forms can be understood in relation to fantasy – to the figuration of desire and sexuality. One will also, inevitably, study a life but it will be in the process of analysing the movement across narrative, plot, character, language. For it is that movement, that interweaving of forms, which constitutes the writer as it constitutes the text.

# 2

# The End of a Meta-Language:
# From George Eliot to *Dubliners*

In order to carry out its task of interpretation, the discourse of
literary criticism must always be able to identify what is represented, independently of the form of the representation. This
identification is only possible if the discourse of the critic is in a
position to transform the text into content, and, to undertake
this transformation, the relation between the language of the
text and the language of the critic must be that which obtains
between an object- and a meta-language. A meta-language
'talks about' an object-language and transforms it into content
by naming the object-language (accomplished through the use
of inverted commas) and thus being able to identify both the
object-language and its area of application.[1] It is from the position of the meta-language that correspondence between word
and world can be established.

A text is made up of many languages, or discourses, and the
critic's ability to homogenise these articulations is related to

[1] The definition of a meta-language is taken from Tarski's classic article on
the semantic conception of truth (Tarski 1949). Throughout this work language (and its compounds) will be used as a synonym for discourse, that is to
say as a term to refer to any system of lexical combination which has as effect a
distinct subject position. It is thus not synonymous (except where the context
demands it) with that everyday use of the word 'language' to refer to different
national tongues, nor to Saussure's definition of language (*la langue*) as a
system of differences, a definition which ignores any reference to subject position. An everyday use which approaches closely the sense desired can be
identified in a phrase like 'They speak a different language', when the speaker
is indicating differences of position and attitude amongst speakers of a single
national language.

13

their prior organisation within the text. Joyce's texts refuse the very category of meta-language and a critical discourse is thus unable to obtain any purchase on the text. None of the discourses which circulate in *Finnegans Wake* or *Ulysses* can master or make sense of the others and there is, therefore, no possibility of the critic articulating his or her reading as an elaboration of a dominant position within the text. In Joyce's writing, indeed, all positions are constantly threatened with dissolution into the play of language. The critic cannot grasp the content of Joyce's texts, for the texts investigate the very processes which produce both content and form, object-languages and meta-language.

The absence of a meta-language in Joyce's work is evident in his refusal, a refusal which dates from his earliest writings, to use what he called 'perverted commas' (letter to Harriet Shaw Weaver, 11 July 1924). While those sections in a work which are contained in inverted commas may offer different ways of regarding and analysing the world, they are negated as real alternatives by the unspoken prose that surrounds and controls them. The narrative prose is the meta-language that can state all the truths in the object-language(s) (the marks held in inverted commas) and can also explain the relation of the object-language to the world. This relation of dominance allows the meta-language to understand how the object discourses obscurely figure truths which find clear expression in the meta-language. A meta-language regards its object discourses as material but itself as transparent. And this transparency allows the identity of things to shine through the window of words in the unspoken narrative whereas the spoken discourses which clothe meaning with material are necessarily obscure. At all costs the meta-language must refuse to admit its own materiality, for in so far as the meta-language is itself treated as material, it, too, can be re-interpreted; new meanings can be found for it in a further meta-language. The problem of the infinite regress of meta-languages brings us to the heart of the problem of meaning and interpretation. What the materiality of language constantly insists on, and what is insistently repressed in our society, is the separation between speech (or writing) and consciousness. This separation can be understood as the gap between the act of saying and what is said; a gap which occurs both temporally and spatially. For the time that it takes to traverse a page or listen to a sentence forbids any instantaneous grasping of meaning. Interpretation is perpetually deferred as each segment of meaning is defined by what follows. And in the space that separates eye from page or ear from mouth, there is a constant possibility of an interference, a misunderstanding, that similarly disrupts the presence of meaning. The problem arises from the fact that meaning is distributed through material and is constantly, therefore, open to further interpretations, even though as we say or write a sentence the meaning seems fixed and evident. This formulation of the problem is itself misleading because it presupposes an original moment when there is strict coincidence between meaning and material. The difficulty is more radical because there is no such original moment. The act of enunciation and what is enounced, the saying and the said, are always separated.

It is to ignore this separation that a text uses inverted commas. The meta-language within such a text refuses to acknowledge its own status as writing – as marks of material difference distributed through time and space. The text outside the area of inverted commas claims to be the product of no articulation, it claims to be unwritten. This unwritten text can then attempt to staunch the haemorrhage of interpretations threatened by the material of language. Whereas other discourses within the text are considered as materials which are open to reinterpretation, the narrative discourse functions simply as a window on reality. This relationship between discourses can be taken as the defining feature of the *classic realist text*. The normal criterion for realism (whether a discourse is fully adequate to the real) merely accepts the conception of the real which the classic realist text proposes for its own project. Thus a traditional anti-realist position that no discourse can ever be adequate to the multifarious nature of the real assumes the classic realist division of language and reality. The classic realist text should not, however, be understood in terms of some homology to the order of things but as a specific hierarchy of discourses which places the reader in a position of dominance with regard to the stories and characters. However, this position is only achieved at the cost of a certain fixation, a certain subjection. George Eliot's texts provide an example of this discursive organisation.

In the scene in *Middlemarch* where Mr Brooke goes to visit Dagley's farm we are presented with two discourses. One is the educated, well-meaning, but not very intelligent discourse of Mr Brooke and the other is the uneducated, violent and very nearly unintelligible discourse of the drunken Dagley. But the whole dialogue is surrounded by a meta-language (which being unspoken is also unwritten) which places these discourses in inverted commas and can thereby discuss their relation to truth – a truth illuminatingly revealed in the meta-language. The meta-language reduces the object languages into a simple division between form and content and extracts the meaningful content from the useless form. Thus we find the following passage towards the end of the chapter:

He [Mr Brooke] had never been insulted on his own land before, and had been inclined to regard himself as a general favourite (we are all apt to do so, when we think of our own amiability more than of what other people are likely to want of us). When he had quarrelled with Caleb Garth twelve years before he had thought that the tenants would be pleased at the landlord's taking everything into his own hands.

Some who follow the narrative of his experience may wonder at the midnight darkness of Mr Dagley; but nothing was easier in those times than for an hereditary farmer of his grade to be ignorant, in spite somehow of having a rector in the twin parish who was a gentleman to the backbone, a curate nearer at hand who preached more learnedly than the rector, a landlord who had gone into everything, especially fine art and social improvement, and all the lights of Middlemarch only three miles off (George Eliot 1880, vol. 2, p. 188).

In this passage we are given the necessary interpretations for the discourses that we have just read. The words of Dagley and Mr Brooke are revealed as springing from two types of ignorance which the meta-language can expose and reveal. Thus we have Mr Brooke's attitude to his tenants contrasted with the reality which is available to us through the narrative prose. No discourse, except that charged with the narrative, is allowed to speak for itself, instead each speech must be placed in a context which will reduce it to a simple explicable content. The claim of the narrative prose to grant direct access to a final reality guarantees the claim of the realist novel to represent the invariable features of humanity. To reveal the truth about Mr Brooke permits the generalisations about human nature.

But it is not only the vanity of Mr Brooke that is laid bare; there is also the 'midnight darkness' of drunken Dagley. The metaphor employed contrasts the darkness of Dagley's discourse with the daylight clarity of the prose that surrounds and interprets it. Dagley's darkness has already been indicated through the attempt to render his accent phonetically. The emphasis on the material sounds of Dagley's discourse is directly in proportion to the difficulty in understanding it. The material of language is essentially a material that obscures. It is in so far as the narrative prose is not material that the truths of the world can shine through it.

The irony of the passage, which expresses its mock astonishment at the fact of Mr Dagley's ignorance when surrounded by such illuminating figures (and having 'all the lights of Middlemarch' only three miles away), works through the knowledge that the text has already conveyed and in no way damages the narrative's claim to be representing reality without intermediaries. There is a kind of irony (we will come to it later in our reading of Joyce) which works without any fixed rules for re-writing the ironic passage. This lack of interpretative rules is what makes for the difficulty of reading Joyce's texts. However, in this example from George Eliot we can read an example of classical irony. Classical irony is established in the distance between the original sentence and the sentence as it should be, given the knowledge of reality that the text has already conferred on us. For readers there is no astonishment that such midnight darkness as Mr Dagley's should exist not three miles from Middlemarch because the lights of that town have been exposed as shadows by the greater light of the text itself.

The conviction that the real can be displayed and examined through a perfectly transparent language is evident in George Eliot's Prelude to *Middlemarch*. In that Prelude she talks of those who care 'to know the history of man, and how the mysterious mixture behaves under the varying experiments of Time' and this language of empiricism runs through the text. The view of science as a matter of experiment is of a piece with a view of the immutable quality of human nature. For as language disappears and absents itself from the stage, we can clearly see the two-faced character Janus, the god of communication, one face that of human nature and the other that of the external physical world. To transform language into pure communicative absence is to transform the world into a self-evident reality where, in order to discover truth, we have only to use our eyes. This complete refusal to interrogate the form of the investigation, the belief in language's transparency, is evident on those occasions (frequent enough) when George Eliot reflects on that form. Thus in *Middlemarch* at the beginning of Chapter 15:

A great historian, as he insisted on calling himself, who had the happiness to be dead a hundred and twenty years ago, and so to take his place among the colossi whose huge legs our living pettiness is observed to walk under, glories in his copious remarks and digressions as the least imitable part of his work, and especially in those initial chapters to the successive books of his history, where he seems to bring his armchair to the proscenium and chat with us in all the lusty ease of his fine English. But Fielding lived when the days were longer (for time, like money, is measured by our needs), when summer afternoons were spacious, and the clock ticked slowly in the winter evenings. We belated historians must not linger after his example, and if we did so, it is probable that our chat would be thin and eager, as if delivered from a camp-stool in a parrot-house. I at least have so much to do in unravelling certain human lots, and seeing how they were woven and interwoven, that all the light I can command must be concentrated on this particular web, and not dispersed over the tempting range of relevancies called the universe (George Eliot 1880, vol. 1, pp. 213–214).

Although, at first sight, George Eliot would appear to be questioning her form, the force of the passage is to leave us convinced that we have finally abandoned forms to be treated to the simple unravelling of the real. Fielding's digressions, which, as it were, placed his fictions as fictions, are held to have been due to the 'lusty ease of his fine English'; that is, to a certain style. It should not go unremarked that George Eliot considers pleasure ('lusty ease' in language) as fatal as materiality to the transparency of language. If Fielding insisted on calling himself an historian, the passage demonstrates to us the impossibility of that claim. No author so preoccupied with his own position on the stage, 'the proscenium', can avoid the materiality and pleasure of language. It is only 'we belated historians' who no longer have any style, whose chat 'would be thin and eager', it is only such as these who can unravel the real.

The digression itself is no real digression because, situated in the middle of the narrative, its function is merely to efface itself; to testify to the reality of the story in which it is held. Where in Fielding the digression testifies to the written nature of the work, situating the narrative as construction, in Eliot the digression situates the narrative as pure representation, in which the author could not interfere because the author can no longer speak. In the same way the disclaimer of the 'tempting range of relevancies called the universe' does not affect the narrative's claim to be representing the world as it really is as long as the particular 'web' is fully illuminated. And significantly, once again, we find the metaphor of 'light', which is what the text is going to produce. These disclaimers have the function of ensuring, like the wealth of irrelevant detail which is heaped up in the text, the innocence and absence of a form and a language in which content might be distorted. We are persuaded that language and form have disappeared, allowing light to shine on the previously obscured world. Another example of the same kind of effect can be found in *Daniel Deronda*:

> She spoke with dignity and looked straight at Grandcourt, whose long, narrow, impenetrable eyes met hers, and mysteriously arrested them: mysteriously; for the subtly-varied drama between man and woman is often such as can hardly be rendered in words put together like dominoes, according to obvious fixed marks. The word of all work Love will no more express the myriad modes of mutual attraction, than the word Thought can tell you what is passing through your neighbour's mind. It would be hard to tell on which side – Gwendolen's or Grandcourt's – the influence was more mixed. At that moment his strongest wish was to be completely master of this creature – this piquant combination of maidenliness and mischief: that she knew things which had made her start away from him, spurred him to triumph over that repugnance; and he was believing that he should triumph. And she – ah, piteous equality in the need to dominate! – she was overcome like the thirsty one who is drawn towards the seeming water in the desert, overcome by the suffused sense that here in this man's homage to her lay the rescue from helpless subjection to an oppressive lot (George Eliot 1880, vol. 2, pp. 38–9).

Once again, the objections against the form of describing reality, 'the obvious fixed marks' of writing are swept away as we get taken beyond that 'word of all work Love' to be presented with the very mystery of the drama. The spectre of words deforming reality is raised only to be dissolved by the rising sun of the prose, a very common strategy in realist novels of the nineteenth century where within the realist, and hence unwritten, text the common example of that which is most unreal is the novel, the written text.

It would be a distortion to consider George Eliot's texts as totally determined by that discursive organisation that I have defined as the classic realist text. Within her novels there are always images which counter the flat and univocal process which is the showing forth of the real. Casaubon's key to all the mythologies, Romola's blind father and, perhaps most powerfully of all, the Hebrew language which rests uninvestigable at the centre of *Daniel Deronda*, question and hold in suspense the project of Eliot's texts. Romola's blind father, who stands in the same relation to the girl as does the author – the relationship of creator – reveals metaphorically within the text the inability of the author to see the world that she is creating. The impossibility of writing an historical novel is thereby admitted at one level of the text while, at another, the meta-discourse tries to deny the distance between itself and the discourses of the fifteenth-century Florentine burghers. Similarly Deronda's discovery of the Jewish language and the poems of Mordecai trouble the meta-language in so far as the Jewish language constitutes an area outside its control. Deronda hears the news that Mordecai's work is in Hebrew and untranslatable with 'anxiety'. Such a feeling is not surprising when we recognise that the poems constitute a fatal threat to the meta-language. Confronted with a discourse that it cannot transform into an object (that it cannot name) the meta-language forfeits control of the novel. This lack of control has caused anxiety amongst the readers as well as the characters of *Daniel Deronda*.

The problems and method of reading a realist text may be usefully compared to the problems an analyst faces in the analysis of a neurotic's discourses and the methods used to disengage significant interpretations from those discourses. Conflicts within the psyche combine and interact to produce dreams, symptoms, slips, etc. These psychic productions are described and explained by the neurotic in discourses which render the dreams coherent, the symptoms rational and the slips insignificant. The analyst is invited to offer the neurotic alternative explanations within these explanatory discourses. The analyst, however, has, as it were, to disengage the symptoms and the dreams from these explanatory discourses. Such a disengagement will demonstrate to the analysand not only how the conflicts have entered into the elaboration of the explanatory discourses but more importantly how the major conflict of neurosis can be located within the relationship between the explanatory discourses and the dreams, symptoms or slips.

Let us take, for example, the analysis of dreams and examine the formal structure of that analysis, remembering that this formal structure is realised in the analytic situation as a complex and dialectical process in which each element of the analysis interacts with the others. The patient relates a dream that sounds coherent. Starting from that element in the dream which lacks the coherence of the rest of the material (this might be an addition or a hesitation), the analyst attempts to disengage the dream from the operations of the secondary revision. The secondary revision renders coherent the material produced by the primary operations of the dream work (*displacement* and *condensation* limited by *considerations of representability*). The secondary revision thus provides the dream's own explanatory discourse. Therefore, when the analyst has stripped away the operations of the secondary revision from the dream, the dream has been transformed and it is this already transformed material which forms the basis for the next stage of the analysis.

In the course of an analysis certain key conflicts will repeat themselves. These conflicts are the result of unconscious desires which are denied access to consciousness. But, if the desires do not appear, their absence does. It is the gaps in the narrative of the dream that make evident the working of a censorship which suppresses those elements of the dream that would carry traces of the unconscious desires into consciousness. But the gaps themselves bear witness to an activity of repression and the existence of unconscious desire and it is in an attempt to refuse even the testimony of silence that the secondary revision recasts the dream in a new, coherent form. Now these unconscious desires will none the less affect the form and content of the secondary revision but, more importantly, it is in the need of the secondary revision to accomplish its work that one can locate the fundamental neurotic conflict. Independently of the content of the particular neurosis, one could aphoristically describe the condition of the neurotic as the refusal to recognise the existence of the unconscious.

This refusal naturally produces two stages within the neurotic's repression of the workings of the unconscious. We have the original repression of the desire because it is unacceptable to consciousness and then we have the further repression of the evidence of the original repression. The analyst, therefore, attempts in one and the same moment to bring the existence of unconscious desire to the attention of the neurotic and to persuade the neurotic to abandon those explanatory discourses which would link all the results of repression to reality. For the neurotic has constant recourse to reality in order to provide a coherent explanation of the troubling symptoms and slips, dreams and parapraxes that compose his or her being.

One can suggest how this comparison can be used to read a realist text by a further brief consideration of one of George Eliot's novels. One can regard the discrete events and dialogues of the story as the original psychic productions and the narrative as the secondary revision which welds these elements into a coherent whole. An analysis of the story of Daniel in *Daniel Deronda* can indicate, if not fully explain, the constitutive relation between the repression of content and the production of form.

Given the importance of the meta-language within Eliot's text, we could pick on the Hebrew language, which cannot be turned into content, as a moment of weakness within the text's coherence. At the start of the novel Daniel Deronda is under kindly pressure from his guardian, Sir Hugo, to choose a career, but he is strangely reluctant to make a decision. In the course of his deliberations he encounters, and becomes fascinated with, the strange and intense character of Mordecai. He is determined to read Mordecai's poetry but Mordecai informs him that it is written in Hebrew and is untranslatable. Daniel, however, learns the language and late in the book, when he meets his mother and learns that he is a Jew, this strange interest in Hebrew is validated. At this point he can justifiably refuse his guardian's request to choose a profession, and he leaves England for Palestine to find a new life and a new state.

Ignoring the rationality of the narrative, we can understand the Hebrew language as significant not because Deronda *really* is a Jew but because it offers, as imaginary mother-tongue, the undifferentiated plenitude which is an escape from the law of the father. The law of the father attempts to impose difference and loss on the son, but, in this case, it can be ignored by Daniel because Sir Hugo is not *really* his father. Within English and England, Deronda must choose a career. Such a choice means defining himself in terms of difference. The mother, however, holds out the promise of a future without loss, for, in Israel, his full being will flower. This escape from the domination of the father (the law of difference signalled by the possession or non-possession of the phallus) is also the crucial articulation in the story of Gwendolen's conflict with Grandcourt, that Victorian struggle between the sexes. For what is Grandcourt's ambition but to define Gwendolen and what is Gwendolen's response but to kill Grandcourt (of course, she does not *really* kill him)?

In the text of *Daniel Deronda*, we can read the desire to transgress the law of the father but, at the same time, the constant disavowal of that desire through an appeal to reality. This appeal is guaranteed by the privileged status of the language charged with the narrative. Narrative *works*, but its workings are repressed by the text's internal discursive relations. Only one language is absolved from any connection with the material of sound or the pleasure of style and it is that language which tells us what is *really* happening. This appeal to the real and the belief in the transparency of language weave the very text of neurosis ensuring the repression of desire. The neurotic refuses to accept that meanings, both sexual and linguistic, are constituted by difference, and, instead, demands constant identities uncontaminated by the world of absence and loss. It is the same refusal and the same demand that dictate the meta-language of realism.

The existence of a meta-language within the text allows the reader (and critic) to read from a position of dominance. It is not necessary for the reader to accept the identifications of the meta-language as long as he or she accepts its position. It is the position that is essential to this textual organisation and not the particular content that is given to reality. It is possible, however, as has already been suggested, to read against the position of the meta-language. To undertake such a challenge is to read against the alibi of reality and to enter into the world of fantasy where language figures and re-figures desire; where the letter is inscribed in the sex and the sex in the letter. It is such a reading that Joyce's texts invite.

Before turning to Joyce, however, it is necessary to emphasise the partial nature of the reading of *Daniel Deronda*. If we take the model of the analyst and the neurotic seriously then it is obvious that it will be necessary to return again and again to the original text (as the analyst returns to the original dream) in order to seek fresh gaps in the narrative with which the text can be re-read. On each occasion the interpretation will be determined by whether the desire uncovered can be located in many parts of the text, not least within the narrative itself. For if such an analysis starts by ignoring the rationality of the narrative, it will finally need to give an account of it.

These considerations raise a final theoretical problem which must be faced before addressing Joyce's texts. Signifying systems of any complexity generate texts which are susceptible to a practical infinity of readings. Psycho-analysis locates the limit on interpretations not in any feature of the dream but in the progress of the analysis. The correctness of an interpretation is not in terms of an ideal homology but in the process of the cure. It is the extent to which an interpretation provokes new material that it will validate itself. But, given this process of validation, it is clear that psycho-analysis's use of the term 'interpretation' bears little relation to classical uses of the same term. Further, it leaves us with the problem of how, outside the process of the cure, we can determine the limits on readings of literature.

The obvious answer, which would grant some ontological status to the text over and above its physical existence, has the unfortunate effect of granting to a text just that identity on which literary criticism depends. On the other hand, to dissolve the text into its readings would seem to leave the way open for voluntaristic appropriations of the most paranoid kind. The way out of this dilemma is to recognise the institutional *weight* of certain readings. George Eliot's texts can be read as classic realism not only because they allow that possibility but because they have been formed institutionally not only in the universities but also, more generally, in those multitudes of contemporary practices which reproduce and sustain an ideology of realism. In analysing literature one is engaged in a battle of readings, not chosen voluntaristically but determined institutionally. The validity of the interpretation is determined in the present in the political struggle over literature. Benjamin recognised this relation between present and past when he wrote, over forty years ago:

> To articulate the past historically does not mean to recognise it 'the way it really was' (Ranke). It means to seize hold of a memory as it flashes up at a moment of danger. Historical materialism wishes to retain that image of the past which unexpectedly appears to man singled out by history at a moment of danger. The danger affects both the content of the tradition and its receivers. The same threat hangs over both: that of becoming a tool of the ruling classes. In every era, the attempt must be made anew to wrest tradition away from a conformism that is about to overpower it (Benjamin 1973, p. 257).

Benjamin's understanding of the determination of the present on the past should not be read as a call for political reductionism. In each practice there will be specific features independently of any political determination and each practice will enter into specific relations *both* with other practices *and* with its political determinations. Above all it must be remembered that the content of politics is not given in terms of any specific representations, let alone those which predominate within capitalist society. A political reading of literature (and all readings are political) will not only involve questions about the place of the text within the ideological struggles of the day but will also involve questions about the nature of that ideological struggle. When we talk of literature, we talk not only of the politics of form but also of the form of politics.

What Benjamin alerts us to are the dangers of a history determined by chronology and the necessity to refuse any linear representations of the past. To support the assertion that Joyce's texts break with classic realism, I will advance arguments that may seem historically misplaced. Would it not be possible to read that break in Conrad, in Hardy, in Dickens – one could continue the list in a vertiginous search for a moment of origin. Classic realism, however, exists in the present. To break with it is a contemporary struggle in which we must attend to those images from the past which are summoned in response to the dangers of conformism. That Joyce is the most necessary of those images is the thesis of this book.

Classic realism can never be absolute; the materiality of language ensures there will always be fissures which will disturb the even surface of the text. It is in terms of the multiplicity of such fissures that one might approach the question of the value of an individual text. It is in so far as the text bears witness to its own activity of repression – in so far as the repressed makes a return – that evaluation within classic realism is possible (see Barthes 1970). But whereas we have to read against the meta-language in a realist text, Joyce's texts, without inverted commas, lack any final and privileged discourse within them which dominates the others through its claim of access to the real. If we continue briefly the use of psycho-analytic theory as a model we could say that whereas the realist text is a neurotic discourse, Joyce's texts might be considered as psychotic discourses. For the neurotic attempts to repress certain desires and ignores the compromise formations which find their way into consciousness through an appeal to 'reality', whereas, in the psychotic, the desires dominate the ego and the ego therefore produces discourses which ignore reality (delusions). (Later in this chapter when the analogy is pushed further it will become clear that Joyce's texts are best characterised as perverse rather than neurotic or psychotic.) His earliest prose writings, the *Epiphanies*, lack any appeal to reality which would define what the writing produces. The conversations and situations which make up these brief ten- or twelve-line sketches, lack any accompanying explanation or context. In place of a discourse which attempts to place and situate everything, we have discourses which are determined in their situation by the reader.

And it is within this perspective that we might consider the distinctions that Joyce draws in his youthful paper 'Drama and Life'. Joyce sets himself against a drama which comes complete with its own interpretation and caught within the stereotype of its age, a drama which Joyce describes as purveyor supplying plutocrat with a 'parody of life which the latter digests medicinally in a darkened theatre'. For Joyce, real drama is to be found in works, like those of Ibsen, which give us the pleasure 'not of hearing it read out to us but of reading it for ourselves, piecing the various parts and going closer to see wherever the writing on the parchment is fainter or less legible'. The contrast between a text which determines its own reading and a text which demands an *activity* of reading was central to Joyce from an early age.

The lack of a dominant discourse which places such emphasis on the reader in *Epiphanies* is equally evident in *Dubliners*. In *Dubliners* we can read the banality and paralysis of Dublin. But this reading is accomplished without the writing offering a point of insertion for our own discourses within an agreed hierarchy of dominance. The text works paratactically, simply placing one event after another, with no ability to draw conclusions from this placing. It is important to recognise that these are not stories 'about' Dublin in the sense that Dublin is

an entity understood and referred to outside the text. Rather it
is a question of the reader producing Dublin through the interaction of his own and the text's discourses. The movement of
the text is not that of making clear a reference already defined
and understood; of fixing the sense of an expression. Instead the
text dissolves the simple sense of Dublin as a city, as a context
within which people live their lives, and replaces it with the very
text of paralysis. It is for this reason that Joyce could talk of a
'special odour of corruption which, I hope, *floats* over my stories' (letter to Grant Richards, 15 October 1905; my emphasis)
and in this 'floating' we have the specific refusal of a fixed sense
which is conveyed by the text. There is no single message
inscribed in the code and the meaning of the text is produced by
the reader's own activity although the text determines that a
certain odour of corruption will float, always in suspension,
over any such meaning. 'Ivy Day in the Committee Room' is an
example of a story which allows the reader no purchase on the
text. The refusal of the narrative to do more than report spatial
positions, or give information strictly relevant to what is happening from moment to moment, leaves the dialogue between
the various occupants of the committee room suspended in a
vacuum of sense, a vacuum that must be filled by the reader.
Parnell simply becomes a function of the text; held in play between the various dialogues. The discourse charged with the
narrative offers no move outside the committee room which
will give the sense of Parnell or the dialogues that turn about
his name.

Although the narrative assumes a degree of control in the
interstices of the dialogue, it is instructive to reflect on some of
the methods with which it interrogates and negates that control. And this negation has nothing to do with the effacement
at work in a realist text but is a process through which the
possibility of a meta-language is systematically ruined. The
story opens with a banal description of a committee room in
which canvassers are resting from their less than arduous
labours. Two of them, Hynes and O'Connor, have ivy leaves
in their lapels and this detail, together with the title, set up an

expectation that these emblems of Parnellism will provide the basis for the control of the story. Standing out from the flat level of the text in which what is described is quotidian and unsurprising, they provide a hermeneutic basis for a controlling political discourse. The reasons why these men have elected to sport these political badges will give meaning to the events in the committee room. Further, the text's ability to produce this meaning will provide the political position for the text's analysis of Irish politics. The text, however, refuses to offer any explanation which transcends the ordinariness of the room and all discussion of politics is locked within the same confines. Nobody will tell us whose side we should be on.

The one occasion when the narrative abandons description for explanation is particularly revealing. Mr Crofton's silence requires some comment: 'Mr Crofton sat down on a box and looked fixedly at the other bottle on the hob. He was silent for two reasons. The first reason, sufficient in itself, was that he had nothing to say; the second reason was that he considered his companions beneath him' (D 146). Instead of a fragment of dialogue, the reader is confronted in this passage with an explanation of a silence. This explanation, however, does not provide a position from which to read the story, for if the other characters mouth the worn slogans of paralysed politics, Crofton's silence does not offer an alternative for it is, itself, the stereotyped response of a Conservative confronted by such nationalist rabble. And it is in terms of stereotype that we can situate the ambiguous nature of *Dubliners*. These short stories function as collections of stereotypes without any discourse that will contain or resolve them. The narrative, in its refusal of a discourse which will explain everything, resists the reduction of the various discourses to one discourse shared by author and reader. Indeed, indirect free style is nothing more than this refusal of agreement between text and reader. Other stories in *Dubliners* may appear to use more traditionally realistic devices, the narrative will go behind a set of actions and explain them. But these explanations use the same cadences and oppositions that characterise some character's speech and they thus refuse any hierarchy of dominance into which the reader could comfortably insert himself. The position we take with regard to the discourses of the text is not mapped out for us and as a result there is no unquestioned discourse in which we can comfortably read the repetition of our 'evident' selves and our 'evident' reality.

The final sentence of the story, 'Mr Crofton said it was a very fine piece of writing', reproduces the whole ambiguity of the text. For the first time someone's words are reported in indirect speech and, with this move, the language of the text, for the first time, masters the discourses of the characters. But this mastery, coming in the final sentence of the text, makes no point which would give us the meaning of the story and, while testifying to its power at a formal level, simply emphasises the lack of a position from which we can read Hynes' poem on the death of Parnell. And this inability to read the poem is, also, the inability to read the story. If we knew whether the poem should be read as yet more cliché in the eternal barrenness of Irish politics or whether it testifies to the enduring reality of Parnell as Ireland's only vital political force then we should know how to make sense of the text. It is in this context that one might profitably compare the irony engendered by Joyce's texts with the more classical irony employed by George Eliot. While we know exactly how to re-write George Eliot's mock surprise about Dagley's ignorance, for the text has repeatedly portrayed the difference between the reality of Middlemarch and Middlemarch's image of itself, it is almost impossible to re-write Crofton's final statement. And this impossibility is the result of the text refusing to provide a discourse which can re-write other discourses. Joyce's writing will only copy down a set of discourses and we are, therefore, forced to rely on our own discourses to re-write and order the text. This personal re-writing is made explicit because we must situate our discourses as dominant; the text will not undertake this situation for us. And in that moment when we become aware of the imposition of our discourses on the text, we also become aware of the stereotype within our own discourses. The agreements which we presume and never question make their appearance at that point where the agreements no longer operate. *Dubliners* generates, through this lack of a meta-language, an endless irony between the stereotypes of the canvassers in the committee room and the stereotypes of our own discourses. Where in the realist text we find a meta-language controlling the other discourses (and it must be emphasised that it is the position of the meta-language that matters and not its content), in *Dubliners* we read the various discourses which constituted a city at a given historical moment and which, besides their contemporaneity, escape any unifying force other than the discourses of the reader.

It could reasonably be objected that the persistence of the 'odour of corruption' remains unintelligible in this account of *Dubliners*. But the odour of corruption is the result of the dominance of stereotype. It is this dominance which paralyses the subject in his or her discourses and allows no fresh articulation to desire. It is this paralysis that seizes hold of Eveline on the quay. Eveline is unable to escape from a life of servitude to her father because finally she cannot allow herself to be defined except in terms of the demands addressed to her by her father. But in so far as she is defined by these demands, in so far as they provide the only articulation of her experience, she cannot find any space in which her own desire could speak. It is no wonder that she is speechless at the end because the paralysis which freezes her in her tracks is a linguistic disorder. But if, in the fixity of stereotypes, we can locate the source of that odour of corruption which arises from the frustration of desire,[1] the reader is not placed within those stereotypes but moves across their contours and this movement, this experience of language, provides the experience of perversion, the reverse coin of neu-

[1] By an exemplary coincidence Moustafa Safouan uses the same metaphor in an attempt to describe the sensations of a psycho-analyst when he or she first listens to a neurotic patient: 'Et quand, de réponse en réponse, une odeur se lève . . . qui n'est plus de déchet mais de pourriture, qu'est-ce qu'il reste comme issue? Rien d'autre que ce qui a déterminé l'entrée.' ('And when, from reply to reply, an odour rises up . . . which is no longer that of waste but of corruption, what is left as a way out? Nothing else but that which determined the way in.') (Safouan 1968, p. 297)

rosis. Freud often talked of neuroses as the negative of perversions and Joyce's early writing is perhaps best defined as perverse.

The perverse nature of the Joycean text is evident in 'The Sisters', the opening story of *Dubliners*. It is interesting, for our purposes, to compare the two surviving versions of this story about a young boy's reactions to the death of the priest, Fr Flynn. In the first version of the text, which was printed in the *Irish Homestead* in 1904, we can find most of the details that appeared in the published version. What are almost entirely missing from the former, however, are the reflections of the 'I' persona over and above his immediate reactions. A comparison of the opening paragraph illustrates the changes:

(1) Three nights in succession I had found myself in Great Britain Street at that hour, as if by Providence. Three nights also I had raised my eyes to that lighted square of window and speculated. I seemed to understand that it would occur at night. But in spite of the Providence that had led my feet, and in spite of the reverent curiosity of my eyes, I had discovered nothing. Each night the square was lighted in some way, faintly and evenly. It was not the light of candles so far as I could see. Therefore it had not yet occurred (*Irish Homestead*).

(2) There was no hope for him this time: it was the third stroke. Night after night I had passed the house (it was vacation time) and studied the lighted square of window: and night after night I had found it lighted in the same way, faintly and evenly. If he was dead, I thought, I would see the reflection of candles on the darkened blind, for I knew that two candles must be set at the head of the corpse. He had often said to me: *I am not long for this world*, and I had thought his words idle. Now I knew they were true. Every night as I gazed up at the window I said softly to myself the word *paralysis*. It had always sounded strangely in my ears like the word *gnomon* in Euclid and the word *simony* in the Catechism. But now it sounded to me like the name of some maleficent

and sinful being. It filled me with fear, and yet I longed to be nearer to it and to look upon its deadly work (D 7).

In the second text the theme of paralysis is introduced and this word together with 'gnomon' and 'simony' provide a collection of signifiers which are not determined in their meaning by the text. The difference between the situation of the reader in the first and second text is crucial. In the first passage the reader is placed in a state of ignorance (what is the situation the text is describing? What is the significance of the lights? etc.), but this ignorance is what the rest of the text will dissipate (it is the death of a priest, etc.). In the second text the reader is introduced to a set of signifiers for which there is no interpretation except strangeness and an undefined evil. The opening of the final version of the story displays a certain excess of the power of signification (the production of a surplus of meaning) which occurs again in the second major addition to the revised text when the narrator imagines the dead priest is pursuing him:

But the grey face still followed me. It murmured; and I understood that it desired to confess something. I felt my soul receding into some pleasant and vicious region; and there again I found it waiting for me. It began to confess to me in a murmuring voice and I wondered why it smiled continually and why the lips were so moist with spittle (D 9).

Once again we find a certain excess of meaning in the priest's act of confession. The gap between the utterance, the act of signification (saying, writing) and the proposition, what is signified (said, written), is accentuated and in that gap the reader's own discourses are left to circulate.[1] The emphasis on this gap

---

[1] The distinction between utterance and proposition is captured and related in the French terms *énonciation* and *énoncé*. These two terms take up and recast the Saussurean distinction between *langue* (the systematic differences that allow individual messages to have meaning) and *parole* (those individual messages themselves). In the translator's introduction to the collection of Roland Barthes's essays, entitled *Image-Music-Text*, this shift is glossed as follows: '. . . every *énoncé* is a piece of *parole*; consideration of *énonciation* involves

is what marks the radical difference between the texts of Joyce and those of George Eliot. Where in Joyce's texts the division between signifier and signified becomes an area in which the reader is in (and at) play-producing meaning through his or her own activity, in George Eliot's texts this division is elided at the level of the meta-language. The meta-language attempts to suppress its own activity of signifying (the distribution of signifiers) and to leave a predetermined signified in place. This signified is the evident reality of things, a reality which denies any effectivity to fantasy and language. Because there is an elision of the act of writing and what is written, so, similarly, there is an elision of the act of reading and what is read. Deprived any experience of language, the reader becomes an observer and can ignore the productive effects of his or her discourses.

In our brief analysis of George Eliot's texts, it was argued that the form and content of her novels reproduced the very structure of neurosis. In the search for plenitude undertaken both by Deronda and the meta-language, we can locate the neurotic negation of desire. For desire depends entirely on difference; on the establishment of an object that can be desired in so far as it does not appertain to the subject, in so far as it is radically other. The experience of language as signifier is the condition of existence of desire. For as a word only finds a meaning through the differential relations it enters into, so the object as it is produced by language is always contaminated by absence – by what it is not. It is only with the establishment of absence

not only the social and psychological (i.e. non-linguistic) context of *énoncés*, but also features of *langue* itself, of the ways in which it structures the possibilities of *énonciation* (symbol-indexes such as personal pronouns, tenses, anaphores are the most obvious of these linguistic features of *énonciation*). The distinction – the displacement – has particular importance in any – semiological, psycho-analytical, textual – attention to the passage, the divisions, of the subject in language, in the symbolic, to the slide seized in the disjunction of the *sujet de l'énoncé* and the *sujet de l'énonciation*. In the utterance "I am lying", for example, it is evident that the subject of the proposition is not one with the subject of the enunciation of the proposition – the "I" cannot lie on both planes at once. Dream, lapsus and joke are so many disorders of the regulation of these planes, of the exchange between subject and signifier; as too, exactly, is the *text*' (Barthes 1977, pp. 8–9). In order to avoid the repetition of the French terms I shall use the words 'enunciation' and 'enounced'.

that desire can function. George Eliot's texts are devoted to repressing the operations of the signifier by positing a metalanguage which exists outside of materiality and production. The multitude of objects which appear in her texts do not bear witness to the activity of signification, to the constitutive reality of absence, but rather, in their massive identity, they deny the existence of such activity. And denying this activity, they deny the reality of absence. It is such a denial that constitutes the repression of desire.

Joyce's texts are very different because although the father, the Church, the past, constantly demand an identity outside of signification, the subject can institute difference by splitting her or himself, a split which allows for both absence and desire. George Eliot is concerned with the fixation of the subject in reality. The mother tells Deronda who he is and this identification guarantees the text's ability to identify us as readers and tell us who we really are. In Joyce the split instituted within the subject allows desire to function and leaves the reader unidentified. The splitting of the subject is achieved through the accentuation of the split between enunciation and enounced. This is effected in the text of *Dubliners* by those moments when the reader is no longer assured in his position in the enounced and thus experiences his own discourses as enunciation, as a process of production. The particular signification associated with paralysis (or the act of confession) will be produced by the reader who will thus find himself in the situation of reading his own discourses. This situation, with all that it carries of a fundamental alienation, is the one experienced by the narrator with regard to the word 'paralysis'. 'I said softly to myself the word *paralysis*' – it is in the distance between the speaking and the hearing of the word that desire is instituted – 'I longed to be nearer to it'.

The desire engendered by Joyce's texts is perverse. This perversity is evident at the level of content, for perversion is the fundamental mode of sexuality in Joyce – there is no example of 'normal' sexual intercourse directly represented in his work. Even in *Finnegans Wake* when H.C.E. and A.L.P. copulate in the morning, H.C.E. fails to reach orgasm, as is pointed out in the text by the famous 'You never wet the tea' (585.31). Formally, this perversion is inscribed in the impossibility of finally disrupting the security of reading. Just as the pervert wishes both to admit and deny sexual difference in a complex articulation of disavowal, the reader is *both* submitted to an experience of language *and* maintains the dominant position of reader. The possibility of a meta-language is inscribed in the distance between the language of the text and the language of the reader. Joyce's writing involves ever greater efforts to abolish this distance.

What is essential to grasp in the articulation of Joyce's texts is that there is no position within them where the reading subject can insert itself to consume some paralysed reality. The writing subject, confronted by the ever present demand of this reality to declare its identity and repress desire, institutes desire through splitting itself within the processes of signification. The reading subject must follow the positions taken up by the writing subject and in the split thus instituted can begin to read its own discourses – not as some transparent window onto an evident reality but as a set of significant oppositions in which the subject's world is constituted and in which, if the subject begins to listen attentively to them, it can hear its desire speak. It is this attention to the forms of discourse which characterises Joyce's practice of writing, its displacement from classic realism:

This shift is not to be understood in the traditional terms of a change from 'social realism' to 'psychological realism' or whatever, but in terms of the deconstruction of the very 'innocence' of realism. Its foundation is a profound experience of language and form and the demonstration of that experience in the writing of the novel which, transgressed, is no longer repetition and self-effacement but work and self-presentation as *text*. Its realism is not the mirroring of some 'Reality' but an attention to the forms of intelligibility in which the real is produced, a dramatisation of possibilities of

language, forms of articulation, limitations, of its own hor-
izon (Heath 1972b, p. 22).

What is important about this attention is that it is also,
always, a transformation. In *Dubliners* the banality of everyday
discourse is removed from its quotidian normality and transformed into a text which can be analysed. This analysis cannot,
however, be constructed in terms of some external truth which
the text represents or embodies. Instead we should consider it
in terms of the lines of force that constitute the text and which
engage with those same forces in our own discourse. Truth is no
longer correspondence but struggle.

# 3

# The End of the Story:
## *Stephen Hero* and *A Portrait*

Truth as struggle. No longer is it a question of truth as correspondence but of the *forging* of positions of judgement – the establishment of areas where correspondence is installed. Forgery, here, is the appropriate word capturing elements of both 'force' and 'counterfeit' and it is unsurprising that Joyce was so fascinated with forgery and with the fictitious Victorian forger, Jim the Penman, who provides one of the constant references of *Finnegans Wake*. For the forger understands writing as continuous production rather than natural representation and Joyce's texts participate in that understanding.

Julia Kristeva, within a continuing work on the relations between language and literature, has considered these different conceptions of truth in terms of a distinction between *symbol* and *sign*. The symbol: one-to-one correspondence between word and thing; a correspondence always guaranteed by God in one or other of his guises. The sign: a constantly shifting world where the fundamental discontinuity between signifier and signified hesitates and refuses the movement towards an exterior in order to discover its own systematicity – the area of its own truth (cf. Kristeva 1970, pp. 25–35). The symbol is the guarantee of the realm of simple disjunction: the word either does or does not represent a state of affairs. The exit from this realm (the fall from grace) is the experience of the sign; experience of a world where a system of differences (constantly open to re-articulation) defines the word and where, therefore, the simple either-or is held in a state of *suspension*. The experience and development of the non-disjunctive nature of the sign is, for Kristeva, one of the essential tasks in the struggle against that notion of truth which is handed down to us by Platonism and Christianity, a struggle which already has many fronts:

> L'idéologème du signe, en effet, non-disjonctif et transforma-tionnel, est à la base des grands moments que notre culture a enregistrés. Citons parmi eux: la conception de la négation et de la permutation dialectique chez Hegel et Marx; le développement de la linguistique après Saussure et de la logique après Peirce, c'est-à-dire la constitution de systèmes formels qui n'ont pas de support idéologique, éthique ou véridique en dehors d'eux mêmes mais intègrent leur 'vérité' dans la construction simultanée de leur modèle; et enfin, la constitution de la sémiologie comme nouveau mode de pensée absorbant dans le signe (le modèle) les différents systèms signifiants. (The ideologem of the sign, in effect non-disjunctive and transformational, is at the base of the great moments that our culture has recorded. Amongst them one could cite: the concept of negation and dialectical permuta-tion in Hegel and Marx, the development of linguistics since Saussure and logic since Peirce, that is to say, the con-stitution of formal systems which have no ideological, ethical or veridical support exterior to themselves, but which inte-grate their 'truth' in the simultaneous construction of their model; and finally, the constitution of semiology as a new manner of thinking, absorbing in the sign (the model) the dif-ferent signifying systems.) (Kristeva 1970, p. 190)

More familiarly for us, in an Anglo-Saxon context, it is the work of Wittgenstein which constitutes this reflection on the sign and the consequent change in the location of truth. Michael Dummett has formulated the new organisation of truth thus:

> We are entitled to say that a statement P must be either

true or false, that there must be something in virtue of which either it is true or it is false, only when P is a statement of such a kind that we could in a finite time bring ourselves into a position in which we were justified either in asserting or denying P; that is, when P is an effectively decidable statement (Dummett 1959, p. 160).

Dummett thus rejects a disjunctive analysis of discourse in favour of a non-disjunction which can only be resolved by a 'bringing of ourselves into position'. The elaboration of this play between discourse and position was forced on Wittgenstein after he had proposed, in the *Tractatus Logico-Philosophicus*, what will probably prove to be the last of the great correspondence theories of truth.[1]

Wittgenstein's correspondence theory was original in that it did not involve an homology of word and thing at the level of ordinary speech, for this ordinary speech was a complex function of simpler elementary propositions, the analysis of which was made possible by Frege and Russell's development of the propositional and predicate calculus. Thus a structural homology was asserted which related elementary propositions to states of affairs (*Sachverhalte*). The states of affairs are combinations of simple objects; the elementary propositions concatenations of names (2.01,4.22). Names are considered as that linguistic form whose only relation is to the object it names (a mistake Wittgenstein later identified as a confusion between the bearer of a name and its meaning). Given this one-to-one correspondence between object and name, all that was further needed was a similarity of form between the combination of objects and the concatenation of names. This similarity is understood through a consideration of how a picture represents, a consideration which finds its clearest expression at 2.17: 'What a picture must have in common with reality, in order to be able to depict it – correctly or incorrectly – in the way it does, is its pictorial form.' Similarly in order for language to depict, there must be an identity between the form of lan-

[1] My comments on Wittgenstein are indebted to long conversations with Derek Bolton and Charles Larmore.

guage (logical form) and the form of reality.

The meaning of an elementary proposition is 'given by a condition of reality, a state of affairs, which is the truth-condition of the proposition' (Bolton 1973, p.34) and the truth-conditions are the permutation of the disjunction of a proposition and its negation. This is what allows Derek Bolton to argue that the essential novelty of the *Tractatus* is as follows:

> This simple interdefinability (the fact that all sixteen truth functions of two elementary propositions can be defined using only negation and conjunction i.e., $P \vee Q = df. - (-P \& -Q)$) reminds us that all propositions represent the existence and non-existence of states of affairs. *This* is the central point, to which all the apparatus of truth function theory is only corollary. The theory enables us to express in a clear and advantageous way, the fact that given elementary propositions, we may negate them, and add them together. The novelty is that in specifying the sense of compound propositions we avoid, as it were, fresh reference to reality, to the states of affairs they represent. Instead their sense, what they represent in reality, is given by appeal to the truth conditions of elementary propositions (Bolton 1973, p. 36).

But not only does this anchoring of language in elementary propositions avoid the need to refer to reality again, it also, and more importantly, avoids conceiving of language as a system of signs defined differentially. It establishes the meaning of language as representation and this representation as independent of any inter-linguistic relations. Wittgenstein's doubts about the *Tractatus*, expressed in conversations with the Vienna circle, began when he realised that the discourse of colour, which looked as though it should contain elementary propositions ('This is red' does not suggest the possibility of further analysis), could not, in fact, be defined through a combination of negation and disjunction. 'This is red' does not simply enter into a disjunct with 'This is not red' but implies the statement 'This is not green'. In other words it is impossible to disengage the colour propositions one from another in the way the *Trac-tatus* had envisaged.

This problem prompted Wittgenstein's return to philosophy and the rest of his work constitutes a constant interrogation of language as system and set of heterogeneous systems; an interrogation which takes place at the level of form and content. But although language is considered as system, its systematicity is still something outside experience: 'The system of language is not in the category of experience' (Wittgenstein 1974, p. 170). The only reason we need to pay attention to the systematicity of language is as therapy for the philosophical disease of attempting to reduce that heterogeneous systematicity to one single system. The aim of philosophy, in its new role as therapy, is to lead us back into the areas where language is obvious, where 'the chain of reasons has an end' (Wittgenstein 1964, p. 143), where language becomes transparent within its appropriate practice. This is the 'bringing into position' which Dummett mentioned: a statement becomes effectively decidable within a practice which provides criteria of judgement. What is interesting is that, for Wittgenstein, the perception of language as system, as non-disjunctive discourse, is only needed as a cure for the disease of philosophy. A normal, healthy use of language would always leave one 'in position'. However, it is not simply disease that leads us from position to system for this movement is constantly forced on us by the nature of the sign. Nor is it simply a question of finding those customary non-linguistic practices where discourse becomes transparent and everything is rendered coherent; it is also a question of forging new practices and the discourses appropriate to them. This forging disrupts the coherence that Wittgenstein wished to confer on language and experience. For someone like Michel Foucault, fascinated by the play of language, the bringing of discourse into position, the bringing of interpretations to an end, is an operation of violence rather than a move back into a comfortable order (cf. Foucault 1967, pp. 183–92).[1]

---

[1] Charles Larmore concludes an unpublished paper, entitled 'Use and Representation in Wittgenstein', with the suggestion that Wittgenstein's

Thus while Wittgenstein indicates the non-disjunctive nature of the sign, the experience of this non-disjunction is only understood in terms of a process of sickness and cure. Narration, as we shall see, proposes itself in terms of cure and Wittgenstein chooses narrative as an evident example of how system (discourse) is effaced from experience: 'Certainly I read a story and don't give a hang about any system of language' (Wittgenstein 1974, p. 171). For Wittgenstein, the reading of a story is opposed to an understanding of language as system, a systematicity which lies outside 'the category of experience'. Joyce's texts provide the experience of system, of a discourse which is constantly forging positions, and this is accomplished through a destruction of any possibility of a story which, in its narration, would efface the system of language. It is the coherence of narration that grants us a position outside language and to dissolve that position is to subvert narrative. In the passage just quoted, Wittgenstein goes on to say that 'a sentence in a story gives us the same satisfaction as a picture'. This satisfaction is the escape from the world of language and difference into one of vision and presence. What remains to be analysed is the contradictory functioning of narrative which uses language only to deny its reality.

Our task is to demonstrate how stories exhibit and repress the reality of language; how the non-disjunctive nature of the sign is the condition of existence of narration and how narration necessarily denies that nature. This project involves a rejection of a structuralist approach. Propp and Greimas have formalised, in different ways, an analysis of stories in terms of a set of disjuncts, the permutations of these disjuncts producing action. But in taking those disjuncts as given before the text, they have

---

account of language can be questioned from a psycho-analytic perspective: 'One assumption of any theory of representation, which I have not yet mentioned, and which is apparent throughout Wittgenstein's writings, is what I shall call a certain "egocentrism". The only way I can "live" in a system of signs is that, when the signs efface themselves from perception, in order to show what they represent, it is from *my* perception that they efface themselves. And for this reason, Wittgenstein writes that *I* use a sign. Wittgenstein could never really come to terms with Freud's claim that we can *live* within systems of signs that the perceiving "ego" is not in a position to *use*.'

ignored the process by which disjunction is both asserted and denied, is held in suspension, within narrative. They ignore the process of narration and, in place of a perpetual structuration, they analyse a set of unchanging structures. Julia Kristeva, while recognising the weakness of this traditional structuralist approach, attempted to give it a limited validity for one particular form of textual organisation. She attempted to draw a distinction, historically based, between the *epic* and the *novel*. For Kristeva, the *epic* is organised as a pure combination of oppositions which are given in the ideological world of religion, independently of the text's activity. As readers of an epic we know that the hero is good and the villain bad and that these two worlds cannot overlap and contaminate each other; the disjuncts are constantly maintained in the world of the symbol, guaranteed in their truth by a separate and exterior realm. The *novel* suspends these disjuncts for the course of the narrative – is the hero good or bad? – only to affirm a final identity and with this affirmation to retroactively deny the suspense produced by the narrative. It is evident that traditional structuralist analysis can cope with the first category but that it is unable to cope with the second. It is the second form of textual organisation that interests us, and, without entering into the historical validity of Kristeva's distinction (in later work she has abandoned it), it can provide the basis for a useful classification. For our purposes, let us elaborate on Kristeva's work by distinguishing between *epic*, which is linked to *reporting*, and *classic realism*, which is linked to *narration*.

To narrate is to leave the realm of disjunction, in which we are all in a position to render a statement effectively decidable, and to enter into an experience of language in which the truth or falsehood of a statement is only established from within the text. Signifiers thus escape any final determination as to their signifieds until the end of the narrative. This deferment of meaning opens up the reader to language, to the functioning of the signifier. The liberation of language and the reader is, however, provisional. It is accompanied by the promise that the correct signifieds will be provided by the text and that we will be reassured, in position, outside the movement of language. The contradiction of narrative is that this future promise of position is always the denial of the present reality of liberation, although the promise only makes sense in terms of that very liberation it seeks to deny.

It is Freud's account of the dialectic between pleasure and desire which offers the most effective explanation of the appeal of classic realism. If, on the one hand, there is a tendency towards stasis, towards a normalisation of excitation within the psyche, there is also a compulsion to repeat those moments at which the stasis is set in motion, at which the level of excitation rises to unbearable heights. The small boy in *Beyond the Pleasure Principle* in his endless game of *fort-da*, ceaselessly throws away the object at the end of the string only to draw it back and start again. This action, which Freud tells us reproduces the experience of separation from the mother, shows that it is exactly the moment of anxiety, of heightened tension, the moment of coming which is relived in a constant cycle which threatens life itself. Classic realism disrupts the position of pleasure only to reassure us of its return, it is this gap which produces the heightened tension we experience as narrative. Classic realism is thus caught in a constitutive contradiction between the elaboration of non-disjunction and the denial of this elaboration, between the experience of difference and the denial of that experience. In classic realism, the elaboration of truth as struggle between text and performer (writer or reader) goes together with the desperate assertion that the text only exists in correspondence to a truth that is given in the world. The classic realist text starts from an incoherence between word and world but this incoherence will be resolved and, furthermore, it has always already been resolved in advance. This constitution of narrative has been described as follows:

The paradox of such a narrative is then this: aimed at containment, it restates heterogeneity as the constant term of its action – if there is symmetry, there is dissymmetry, if there is resolution, there is violence; it contains as one contains an enemy, holding in place but defensively, and the strategic point is the implacable disjunction of narrative and discourse, *énoncé* and *énonciation*, the impossibility of holding entirely on the subject-position of the one the subject-process of the other . . . (Heath 1975a, pp. 49–50).

In its passage from an incoherence to a coherence which is always guaranteed in advance (in its passage from innocence to knowledge, in its passage from confusion to identity), the classic realist text is always the story of lost illusions. Balzac's novel *Illusions perdues* offers us an apt example of the movement of narrative which desires and produces a coherent position but, at the same time, wishes to know nothing of desire and production, for such knowledge would refuse the possibility of any final coherence. Balzac's novel tells the story of two young men, Lucien and David. The story opens with both youths gripped by Romantic ideals but languishing within a small provincial town. Lucien is worshipped by his sister and widowed mother and under the influence of a local aristocrat, Madame de Bargeton, he goes to Paris to realise his artistic vocation. David remains behind condemned to inherit his father's printing works. In Paris Lucien's continual failures are the result of his attachment to his literary illusions and his incapacity to appreciate the realities of life. Even when he forsakes his writing and makes a fortune as a journalist, his success is the result of political intrigues which he does not understand and which finally cast him down as quickly as they raised him up. When Lucien returns penniless from Paris, he finds David prosperous, married to his sister and supporting his mother. After he has almost ruined David, even his mother and sister lose patience with him, and he determines to commit suicide. At this point, when he has lost all his illusions about himself, he is rescued by a character (whom we know, from other texts in *La Comédie humaine*, to be Vautrin) and this anonymous rescuer spells out to Lucien the lessons to be learned from his fate. If these lessons are well-learned, if he has lost his illusions, then Vautrin promises to make Lucien a success in Parisian Society.

The progress of the novel is towards Lucien's identity, but, once reached, this identity becomes retroactively effective, denying the reality of the non-disjunctive world of the text. Lucien's illusions and their fate circulate around his refusal to recognise paternal authority and his narcissistic attachment to his mother and sister. His mother's maiden name was de Rubempré and it is this aristocratic name which Lucien claims for his own rather than accept the paternal and plebeian Chardon. The suspension of the disjunction, Chardon *or* de Rubempré, produces the space of the narrative. Lucien's appearance as Chardon *and* de Rubempré allows the other impossible conjunctions of the text. Symbolically Lucien refuses to renounce the maternal world of infancy *and* yet participates in the paternal world of society, psychologically he is both good *and* bad, honourable *and* dishonourable, historically he is both a real actor in the political events of the 1820s *and* an imaginary actor in his own fantasies. It is these contradictions that the narrative elaborates but always *will have* resolved for although narrative suspends disjunction as its own condition of existence, it is written in a future perfect which denies reality to this suspense.

The narrative closes itself by finding a father for Lucien who will confer the name of de Rubempré. Vautrin, in his promises to Lucien, is the final proof of Lucien's illusory attachment to the reality of the mother. It is as father that Vautrin will make Lucien a de Rubempré:

Je veux aimer ma créature, la façonner, la pétrir à mon usage, afin de l'aimer *comme un père aime son enfant.* Je roulerai dans ton tilbury, mon garçon, je me réjouirai de tes succès auprès des femmes, je dirai: "Ce beau jeune, c'est moi! ce marquis de Rubempré, je l'ai créé et mis au monde aristocratique; sa grandeur est mon oeuvre, il se tait ou parle à ma voix, il me consulte en tout." (I want to love my favourite, to shape and mould him for my enjoyment so that I can love him *as a father loves his child*. I will ride in your tilbury, my boy, I will rejoice in your success with women, I will say: "This handsome young man is me! This marquis de Rubempré, it is I who have created him and introduced him to the aristocratic world; his nobility is my work, he speaks or guards his tongue at my command, he consults me in everything".) (Balzac 1963, vol. 12, p. 553; my emphasis)

It is with the production of a father for Lucien that the text resolves its problems in a moment which also denies the reality of the problem. *Illusions perdues* traverses the classic path of narrative in that it is a desperate attempt to deny sexuality, the knowledge of which provides its first impetus. Philippe Sollers has analysed this denial of sexuality in terms of the creation of a false father:

> Un faux père . . . mis là . . . à seule fin d'éviter fantasmatiquement que la mère n'ait pas le phallus, qu'elle soit génitale, qu'elle jouisse. Ce père est une mère. Phallique. Le père, lui, serait en realité un nom. Mais de cela, nul n'a plus peur que l'idéaliste. (A false father set up for the sole purpose of avoiding phantasmatically the mother not having a phallus, of avoiding her being genital, her *coming*. This father is a mother. Phallic. The father in reality is a name but no one is more afraid of that than the idealist.) Sollers 1974, p. 61)

The *Name of the Father*, which is *the* name without a bearer, is the index of language as system of difference. It is the separation of the name of the father from its bearer that is the crucial event for an entry into the symbolic order, the order of language. The symbolic, for Lacan, refers to the structure of difference that constitutes the possibility of articulation.[1] In so far as

---

[1] This Lacanian use of the term symbolic must not be confused with a more ordinary use, evident in the opening part of this chapter, in which a symbol relates to what it represents. It is this conventional sense which is the one employed by Freud; 'Freud stresses the relation which, however complex the connections may be, unites the symbol and what it represents. For Lacan, on the other hand, it is the structure of the symbolic system which is the main consideration, while the links with what is being symbolised – the element of resemblance or isomorphism, for example – are secondary and impregnated by the Imaginary' (Laplanche and Pontalis 1973, pp. 439–440).

such a world is constantly open to re-articulation, the subject can only figure within it on the condition that the subject is incomplete (and therefore subject to desire). It is the recognition of a possible castration that is the inaugurating moment of the symbolic and this moment is conditional on the recognition that the father cannot bear his name, that he, too, is submitted to a symbolic order. In so far as the father figures in the imaginary register, the register of identification and image, as self-sufficient and complete, he will also figure as adequate to the mother's desire. But by representing the satisfaction of the mother's desire, the imaginary father denies its reality as insatiable, that is to say as desire.

If Vautrin can take up the position of an imaginary father who can unite name and bearer and thus deny the reality of the mother's desire, it is because of the work that the narrative has accomplished to make this place a possibility. And that work is the complementary story of David Séchard. In his passage from the maternal world into which he throws himself at the beginning of the novel (adoration of Lucien with Eve and Madame Chardon) to the paternal world he inhabits at the end (as head of the family he reproves Lucien and is joined in this reproof by Eve and Madame Chardon), David's progress is the condition of Lucien's movement from illusion to reality.[1]

What *Illusions perdues* makes illuminatingly clear is that narrative represses both the reality of language and of women. It is language in excess of meaning, women in excess of any male determination, that produces the disease in the imaginary that narrative attempts to cure. Madame de Bargeton is the original

[1] Balzac's novel does, however, end in some suspense for Lucien has not entirely renounced the feminine world. When he scoffs at Vautrin's offer, he compares himself to Marie Antoinette, and this identification with the feminine, together with the fact that in the welter of surnames which close the text Lucien appears without any family determination, leaves open a final ambiguity. This ambiguity has a double determination. First, as part of a larger text, the narrative must re-introduce a certain suspense to ensure another volume can begin. Second, the inability of the narrative to close itself bears witness to the force of the attachment to the mother, an attachment which is never finally or successfully repressed.

figure of this excess and she erupts into the text as a sexual and linguistic heterogeneity which the narrative must do everything to efface. The surplus of sexuality which the text tells us is the result of an impotent husband finds its outlet in a practically incoherent use of language: 'Elle prodiguait démesurément des superlatifs qui chargeaient sa conversation où les moindres choses prenaient des proportions gigantesques' ('She was immoderately lavish in her use of superlatives which inflated her conversation where the littlest things took on gigantic proportions') (Balzac 1963, vol. 11, p. 214). Balzac emphasises the link between a disordered language and female sexuality when he continues the passage by explaining 'il faut *violer* pour un moment la langue afin de peindre des travers nouveaux que partagent quelques femmes' ('it is necessary to *violate* language momentarily in order to depict the new vices that some women share') (my emphasis). But if the reality of female sexuality threatens language, the narrative is concerned to smooth over this reality and to leave men and meanings uncontaminated by bodies or sounds. Vautrin sums up the progress of the narrative when he asks Lucien if he has understood Otway's *Venice Preserved*: 'As-tu compris cette amitié profonde, d'homme à homme, qui lie Pierre à Jaffier, qui fait pour eux d'une femme une bagatelle et qui change entre eux tous les termes sociaux' ('Have you understood this deep friendship, man to man, which links Pierre to Jaffier, a friendship which, for them, transforms women into bagatelles and which changes between them all social relationships.') (Balzac 1963, vol. 12, p.552). With the production of an imaginary father women are denied any reality over and above that of a medium of exchange between men – they have become bagatelles. It is from the security of this position that the meta-language can dominate the other languages in the text. When, for example, a journalist makes a pun on gold (*l'or*) and Dante's Laura (*Laure*), the text spells out the conceit lest an ambiguity trouble its control of meaning. But the material of language can never be fully repressed and within the meta-language itself we can find a pun with which to read against the text. The climax of Lucien's humiliation in Paris is the publication of a poem (written in Lucien's style) which puns on the meaning of *chardon* as thistle in order to indicate that Lucien's pretensions as to his family name have been exposed. The word, however, also means a 'spike' and this phallic meaning, which is not alluded to in the novel, reveals the father in the text as a name. The proliferation of meaning around *chardon* denies the possibility of ever locking name to bearer, word to meaning in that fixed relation which, at another level, the text asserts.

This articulation of language, narrative and sexuality is not peculiar to *Illusions perdues*. Whether these relations are atemporal or historical may be left indeterminate for the moment; their generality, however, can be read in the early history of psycho-analysis. Freud recognised from the start the reality of female sexuality and early on he wrote, with emphasis, that '*the great majority of severe neuroses in women have their origin in the marriage bed*' (Freud 1895d, 2:246). In his early treatment, however, he expected a story that would fix this sexuality in place instead of attempting to find a voice for what had hitherto been silent. Freud noted that his early case-histories 'read like short stories' (1895d, 2:160) and this is not surprising given his determination to locate his patients' sexuality in relation to a primal traumatic event. This determination constituted a constant demand for identity and meaning, that is to say a constant demand for a story. It is only when Freud realised that these stories must be *listened* to as fantasy that psycho-analysis begins. It is only at that moment when sound breaks through the story, when the signifier escapes determination in narration, that it is possible to unwork repressed desire. The story, in its very form, is the masculine reappropriation of the hysterical. The process of the story is the closure of the heterogeneity of the feminine.

It is in the perspective opened up by a consideration of narrative that we can understand the rupture between *Stephen Hero* and *A Portrait of the Artist as a Young Man*. The first is caught within narration and the classic realist text, the second announces a fresh start, which has no beginning, and offers a rhythmic destruction (deconstruction) of the previous economy of discourse. I have attempted to characterise narrative as the constant movement towards the place of knowledge from which narrative can occur. This paradox ensuring that the narrative has always finished before it begins. Narrative smooths over an incoherence but its success is guaranteed from the start lest the incoherence gain a reality which would block narrative's very operation. The condition of existence of narrative is a simultaneous recognition and denial of the problem of difference; a problem which materialises as one of women and language. This, too, is the condition of existence of *Stephen Hero* but the fact that the text only *just* exists suggests that narrative may be undergoing a profound mutation.

Dublin and Stephen are described from the position of knowledge to which the text tends. But the fact that the story remains unfinished is an index of the difficulty of the construction of this position within the text. The incoherence from which *Stephen Hero* starts cannot finally be resolved into a simple position. Because it lacks not only an end but also a beginning it is impossible to trace the logic of the narrative in its entirety but one can indicate that Emma Clery is one of the moments of that disorder which narrative both elaborates and represses. Emma threatens the coherence of Stephen's world and in the outburst when he confronts her with his desire, we can read the illusions about women which the text will undo. In order to dispel the spectre of difference which the reality of Emma Clery and his mother embody, it is necessary for the text to produce a false father. This false father is Ibsen, and, to bring *Stephen Hero* to an end, we would need a recognition scene in which Ibsen would meet a fugitive Stephen in Europe and make Stephen his spiritual heir. As Emma Clery disrupts that self-sufficient identity which Stephen asserts, so Irish, as mother-tongue, threatens meaning and meta-language, the formal possibility of identity, with sound: 'Stephen found it very (hard) troublesome to pronounce the gutturals but he did the best he could' (SH 65). The task of the narrative is to demonstrate that the Irish language, like Emma, can be comprehended and that, therefore, neither pose a threat to Stephen's identity. These symbolic difficulties receive some resolution with the death of Isabel when a woman is punished for her very being. She had 'acquiesced in the religion of her *mother*' (SH 131; my emphasis) and this comment, together with the fact that Joyce transformed the death of his real *brother* George into the death of his fictional *sister* Isabelle, highlights the symbolic threat posed by femininity. A threat which narrative smooths over with an elaborate denial of the reality of sexual difference.

This denial is the narrative's construction of a position from which the meaning of the mother, in particular, and the feminine, in general, can be fixed. *Stephen Hero* attempts this operation but within the text there are forces at work that ensure its failure. The contradictory elements in *Stephen Hero* are also at work in *Dubliners*. It has been argued that the general strategy of *Dubliners* is the refusal of the production of a privileged discourse against which to read off the other languages of the text. This refusal forces the reader to experience the discourses of the characters as articulation rather than representation; in short, to experience language. This formal strategy breaks down, however, in the two stories in which a mother figures prominently, the text in both these stories is organised in terms of a dominant meta-language. In 'The Boarding House', for example, Mrs Mooney, the mother, is not allowed to speak for herself because the narrative immediately fixes her for the reader. It is information shared between reader and text that enables the narrative to pronounce that 'she dealt with moral problems as a cleaver deals with meat' (D64). This direction on how to understand Mrs Mooney is guaranteed by the reference in the simile back to the butcher's shop where Mrs Mooney started her career. In its use of information already given to make a judgement on a character, the text elaborates a common strategy of classic realism, the knowledge shared by narrative and reader places them in a dominating position vis-à-vis the characters and their discourses. This dominant position is also produced in 'A Mother' where the distance between the language of the narrative and the language of the characters is, once again, greater than in the other stories of *Dubliners*. What is evident in these stories, and in *Stephen Hero*, is that women and, particularly, the mother, cannot be allowed to speak for themselves, they must be subdued in language. It is at the moment when the mother comes into prominence at the level of content that the form regresses to a traditional relation of control. In *Dubliners*, the figure of the mother focuses the resistance to an experience of language and desire which is inscribed in the other stories. But this resistance, this fear of articulating the mother's discourse, is finally dissolved in 'The Dead' where Gabriel Conroy's, and the text's, inability to put women in their place opens up a range of possibilities which allow the abandonment of *Stephen Hero* and the beginning of *A Portrait*. Lily, the servant girl, Miss Ivors, the nationalist, and Gretta, his wife, all refuse the identifications which Gabriel wishes to make. 'The Dead' constantly promises a story which never gets told: neither the events at the Misses Morkan nor the heavy symbolism ever come to anything. Gretta is immune to any attempt to narrativise her and the counterpart of this immunity is the excess of sound with which Lily greets Gabriel. In *Stephen Hero* the 'troublesome' sounds of Irish were dismissed by the narrative but, if Gabriel smiles at 'the three syllables she had given his surname'. (D 201), the text gives them no determination and it is this appearance of an undetermined signifier that entails the end of classic realism and the possibility of women's speech, the possibility of desire. This relation of sound and narrative becomes the literal beginning of *A Portrait*:

Once upon a time and a very good time it was there was a moocow coming down along the road and this moocow that was coming down along the road met a nicens little boy named baby tuckoo. . . .

His father told him that story: his father looked at him through a glass: he had a hairy face.

He was baby tuckoo. The moocow came down the road where Betty Byrne lived: she sold lemon platt.

*O, the wild rose blossoms*

*On the little green place.*

He sang that song. That was his song.

*O, the green wothe botheth.*

When you wet the bed first it is warm then it gets cold. His mother put on the oilsheet. That had the queer smell.

His mother had a nicer smell than his father. She played on the piano the sailor's hornpipe for him to dance. He danced:

*Tralala lala,*
*Tralala tralaladdy,*
*Tralala lala,*
*Tralala lala.* (P. 7)

With this opening we have left the order of classic realism which produces a father and a position in meaning at the expense of the mother and language as sound. The first paragraphs of *A Portrait* offer instead a juxtaposition of quotations which oppose the narrating father who fixes one in place with his look and his story ('he was baby tuckoo') and the mother who opens up language as sound and movement, appealing to the nose and the ear against the identifying eye. In *Stephen Hero*, the fear of the mother's speech determines the production of a meta-language; in *A Portrait*, both the fear and the dominating position are displaced. When, however, *Stephen Hero* is not directly concerned with sexuality, that dominating position is continually undermined. *Stephen Hero* thus exists in a contradiction, the same contradiction that distinguishes in *Dubliners* those stories that focus on a mother from those that do not.

If we return again to the distinction between epic and classic realism and consider the different temporalities that can be inscribed within a text, we will be able to understand how *Stephen Hero* gives way to *A Portrait*. The constant identities within the epic render the enounced separate from the enunciation, for it is not necessary to reach the end of the story to correctly identify the protagonists. The epic can be reported at any time, for the epic is a mere succession of events. In the classic realist text it is the final closing of the non-disjunction in an identity which makes the narration possible: the enunciation is only made possible from the end of the time of the enounced. In classic realism the end of the story becomes the inevitable and necessary condition of the start of the narration whereas in the epic the series of events have no necessary end at all for the report finds its sense and possibility outside the story. Classic realism makes the progression of events internally meaningful and thus introduces time into meaning. The ideology of progress informs both historicist theories of history and the reading of classic realism and we can identify homologies between historicism and classic realism which are not accidental.

Classic realism reproduces two major features of historicism. First, the central concern of the narrative determines every level of the text just as the historicist understands a basic contradiction or essence as determining every aspect of a particular era. Second, classic realism, like historicist history, must be written from a present that has no future for if we are to understand fully all the contradictions (all the suspended disjunctions) then we must stand at the moment of their resolution. This means that nothing from the past can escape the novel because in order to guarantee its own organisation the text must explain everything in the past. It is this necessity that explains *Illusions perdues*'s appropriation of the public realm of events: Lucien's fate is necessarily bound up with the political movements and crises of the 1820s.

*Stephen Hero* is written at the limit of this temporal organisation and *A Portrait* inaugurates a new relation between time and meaning. Classic realism can be understood as working with that division of language characterised by Emile Benveniste in terms of *discourse* and *narrative*. For Benveniste, there is a fundamental distinction to be drawn between that use of language (discourse) in which the speaking subject and an adressee are inscribed – where an 'I' appears which is interchangeable with a 'you' (possibility of identification and exchange) – and a use of language (narrative) in which the speaking subject is not inscribed and 'events that took place at a certain moment of time are presented without any intervention of the speaker in the narration' (Benveniste 1971, p. 206). Benveniste articulates his distinction around the two different forms of the past tense in French – a compound tense used in speech and written communications (the perfect) and an inflection of the verb used in writing which presupposes no addressee (the aorist). Traditionally it has been argued that the use of the aorist in the written language is a simple historical anomaly which will be regulated in time when the perfect replaces the aorist in writing as well as in speech. Benveniste disagrees with this traditional view and argues that the persistence of the aorist is a syntactic index of two different orders of language. There is no such clear syntactic division between discourse and narrative in English and although one might try to organise a division between uses of language in which 'it' or 'there' functioned as an impersonal subject and those in which the verbs are governed by interchangeable personal pronouns, it is doubtful if one could produce any systematic syntactic basis for Benveniste's argument. One can still, however, recognise the usefulness of such a distinction as long as it is also recognised that, at another and deeper level, narrative is already discourse. For in its use of proper names, the impersonal mode of narrative offers the possibility of exchange with pronouns. How 'I' can talk about myself depends on how fiction allots predicates to proper names. In our discourse we are offered positions by narrative and narrative depends on the possibility of this interchange with discourse. The suspense of classic realism is the interplay between these two uses of language, an interplay which is regulated by the assured dominance of narrative. The disjunction between the 'it' of the narrative and the 'I' of the central character provides a constant suspense in the classic realist text but this suspense is predicated on the eventual identity of narrative and discourse at the end and it is from this imaginary point of identity that the story is written. Thus in *Illusions perdues* we move between the narrative that tells us Lucien will fail in Paris and Lucien's discourse which promises success but we rest secure in their eventual congruence. Progress in classic realism is the movement towards a continuous present from which this

temporary present will be understood. To write an account of
the dialectical movement of history we must write from an absolute present.

*Stephen Hero*'s difficulties can be understood as the difficulty
of organising narrative and discourse in this traditional way:

> By all this society liberty was held to be the chief desirable;
> the members of it were fierce democrats. The liberty they
> desired for themselves was mainly a liberty of costume and
> vocabulary: and Stephen could hardly understand how such
> a poor scarecrow of liberty could bring (to their) serious
> human beings to their knees in worship. As in the Daniels'
> household he had seen people playing at being important so
> here he saw people playing at being free. He saw that many
> political absurdities arose from the lack of a just sense of com-
> parison in public men. The orators of this patriotic party
> were not ashamed to cite the precedents of Switzerland and
> France. The intelligent centres of the movement were so
> scantily supplied that the analogies they gave out as exact
> and potent were really analogies built haphazard upon very
> inexact knowledge. The cry of a solitary Frenchman (A bas
> l'Angleterre) at a Celtic reunion in Paris would be made by
> these enthusiasts the subject of a leading article in which
> would be shown the imminence of aid for Ireland from the
> French government. A glowing example was to be found for
> Ireland in the case of Hungary, an example, as these
> patriots imagined, of a long suffering minority, entitled by
> every right of race and justice to a separate freedom, finally
> emancipating itself. In emulation of that achievement
> bodies of young Gaels conflicted murderously in the
> Pheonix Park with whacking hurley sticks, thrice armed in
> their just quarrel since their revolution had been blessed for
> them by the Anointed, and the same bodies were set aflame
> (at) by the unwelcome presence of any young sceptic who
> was aware of the capable aggression of the Magyars upon
> the Latin and Slav and Teutonic populations, greater than
> themselves in number, which are politically allied to them,

and of the potency of a single regiment of infantry to hold in check a town of twenty thousand inhabitants (SH 66–7).

In this passage narrative and discourse do not provide a suspended disjunction which we can confidently expect will be resolved at the end, rather they contaminate each other. Instead of moving between the world of narrative and Lucien's world of discourse, as in *Illusions perdues*, we find in *Stephen Hero* that the narrative is constantly disrupted by Stephen's discourse. The confusion between narrative and discourse, between personal and impersonal, between reality and illusion can be read in the long passage between 'He saw' and 'a young sceptic'. It is impossible to decide whether we have left Stephen's discourse for an impersonal narrative, an indecision confirmed by the shift back in the last six or seven lines when Stephen is placed in the position of political knowledge that one might have assumed to belong to the narrative. This indecision poses a problem of the text's production of a position for the reader. It has been argued that such a position is dependent on the movement between narrative and discourse but in *Stephen Hero* this movement never gets under way.

It could be said that this is simply another way of describing indirect free style. The problem, however, is that the imprecise term of indirect free style covers a variety of discursive organisations. Narrative and discourse may appear to be joined together in any form of first person narration. But if the discourse of the hero at the beginning of the novel is distinct from the narrative that it will become at the end, if, that is to say, the narrative starts by placing a distance between the knowledgeable 'I' that writes and the naive 'I' that must experience in order to write, then it is merely a version of the classic realist text. For it is the determining function of the 'end' of the text that specifies the organisation of classic realism. It is at the moment when the impersonal pronouns of the narrative and the personal pronouns of the hero's discourse are aligned that the possibility of exchange and identification is fully defined. It is this security of position which ensures that all endings are happy. For the end determines every discourse in terms of the evident and extra-linguistic truth or falsity represented by the narrative and thus puts a stop to the uncontrollable substitutions of language. The end of the story ensures we read narrative as representation rather than articulation. (Epic can be distinguished from classic realism in that there is no pressing necessity for an end. Our position vis-à-vis the discourses of the characters is determined by extra-textual truth conditions.)

A discursive organisation which contains no promise of an end reveals its own contours and organisation. Without an end narrative becomes impossible: it is unmasked as discourse *Stephen Hero* constantly reaches towards this new discursive order (different from either epic or classic realism) as narrative collapses into discourse, but, after each collapse, the narrative limps lamely on. It is this which makes *Stephen Hero* such a clumsy book for it cannot generate *suspense*. This failure makes it unsurprising that the text could not be brought to an end.

It is easy to say that the impossibility of divorcing narrative and discourse is the result of a shallow egotism on Joyce's part (one can equally accuse him of a lack of subtlety or failure of sensibility), but this is to ignore a fundamental disorder of discourse by merely concentrating on some of its effects. If discourse is jammed on narrative then clumsiness ensues and this clumsiness reveals itself symptomatically as a difficulty with pronouns. Pronouns are the linguistic condition of identification; one could say that the ability to switch persons is what marks our entry to the human world. *Turpin Hero*, the old English ballad which provides the title for *Stephen Hero* and is discussed in *A Portrait*, can begin in the first and end in the third person because of the interchangeability of pronouns and the resultant possibility of identification and exchange. Classic realism provisionally suspends this interchangeability: in *Illusions perdues*, for example, the 'he' of the narrative and the 'I' of Lucien's discourse are not equivalent. But if the reader is articulated both in Lucien's discourse and the narrative, he or she can rest assured that this double articulation will be synchronised by the end of the text and that this synchronisation will confirm the transparency and security of language. In *Stephen Hero* these possibilities have disappeared. The narrative can dominate the other discourses but it has become conscious of itself as discourse and thus the writing *jars*:

> When a demand for intelligent sympathy goes unanswered he (it) is a too stern disciplinarian who blames himself for having offered a dullard an opportunity to participate in the warmer movements of a more highly organised life. So Stephen regarded his loan of manuscripts as elaborate flag practices with phrases (SH 88).

The hesitation between 'he' and 'it' in this passage indicates the text's uncertainties. The movement from first person to third person in *Turpin Hero* is the guarantee that a content can be fixed for the shifting 'I' in a set of statements about 'he'. In order for the exchange to fix a meaning for the 'I' the set of statements must be enumerable and it is the necessity of their enumerability which is the necessity of an end. This movement from 'I' to 'he' is the possibility of narrative because it establishes an impersonal world independently of the illusion of personal language. It is this independent and agreed world which provides the subject of narrative – the confident and impersonal 'it'. *A Portrait* will move from the third to first person operating a reverse procedure and dissolving narrative into discourse instead of fixing discourse in terms of narrative. *Stephen Hero* works between these two positions for, although the text will attempt to enumerate the set of Stephen's characteristics, it can never exhaust them and therefore it can never produce a closed and agreed world which would provide the basis for the 'it'.

The possibility of ending a story is conditional on the politics of the text. In so far as the text appropriates the public world of events it can only bring the story to an end if it also knows the end of history. Balzac knows that any society which is not a true monarchy will fail, he thus always knows the end. A Marxist writer – and during the period that he was composing *Stephen Hero* and *A Portrait*, Joyce would call himself a socialist – can never posit an end to history.

Without the possibility of an end a writer can only investigate the discourses of the day but this investigation can accomplish, in a radical investigation of our sense, a revolution: the revolution of the word.

If we refer back to the opening section of *A Portrait* we can find that the interplay between narrative and discourse is dramatised in the opening few lines. The narrative told by the father produces the structure which through identification will determine discourse. The position of baby tuckoo within the narrative is the starting-point for the subject's discourse. It is by concentrating on this interchange, on this moment of insertion into narrative, that Joyce allows a voice to what is repressed in that moment: the desire of the mother (both subjective and objective genitive). This opening passage of *A Portrait* lends substance to the juxtaposition with which Roland Barthes ends his famous essay on narrative:

> Bien qu'on n'en sache guère plus sur l'origine du récit que sur celle du langage, on peut raisonnablement avancer que le récit est contemporain du monologue, création, semble-t-il, postérieure à celle du dialogue; en tout cas, sans vouloir forcer l'hypothèse phylogénétique, il peut être significatif que ce soit au même moment (vers l'âge de trois ans) que le petit de l'homme 'invente' à la fois la phrase, le récit et l'Oedipe. (Although we know scarcely more about the origins of narrative than we do about the origins of language, it can reasonably be suggested that narrative is contemporaneous with monologue, a creation seemingly posterior to that of dialogue. At all events, without wanting to strain the phylogenetic hypothesis, it may be significant that it is at the same moment (around the age of three) that the little human 'invents' at once sentence, narrative and the Oedipus) (Barthes 1966, p. 28)

The struggle against narrative is the struggle against the father. *A Portrait* attempts to evade paternal identification and, in that evasion, to let the desire of the mother speak. Counter to the classic realist text, *A Portrait* is the product of the desire to make of the father only a name and thus accede to a chain of differences where one is not fixed to a single point but can come and come and come again.

The problem of *Stephen Hero* is that the neutral narrative is time and again interrupted by discourse and these interruptions destroy the very possibility of narrative. But what is a problem for *Stephen Hero* becomes the constitutive principle of *A Portrait*. Montage of discourses, *A Portrait* refuses to tell us stories. The treatment of Stephen's encounters with the university authorities provides a useful comparison between the two texts. In *Stephen Hero* these encounters are all given strong diegetic motivation in terms of the college authorities' recognition of Stephen's identity as a dangerous rebel. As such these episodes become battles of identities, so many attempts to be recognised by a father. In *A Portrait*, there is no diegetic motivation for Stephen's chance encounter with the dean and in the absence of a story it is system which appears instead of position, discourse instead of narrative. The text can ignore the comfortable order of sentences and concentrate on individual words (*tundish*) and on sound:

– The language in which we are speaking is his before it is mine. How different are the words *home, Christ, ale, master*, on his lips and on mine! I cannot speak or write those words without unrest of spirit. His language, so familiar and so foreign, will always be for me an acquired speech. I have not made or accepted its words. My voice holds them at bay. My soul frets in the shadow of his language (P 194).

Any possible ending, any moment at which identity could be asserted in a submission of discourse to narrative, is repeated and ironised within the text. Thus the heroic end of the first section becomes a good joke for Simon Dedalus to tell in the second and this subversion of any possible end is constant throughout the text. The lack of an ending not only brings language and desire to our attention, it also banishes psychology. For it is the mechanisms of suspended disjunction which allow the possibility of psychological investigation. In *Illusions perdues*, to return to our example, the poet d'Arthez and the journalist Lousteau are represented as two opposing character types. This opposition, however, is suspended in Lucien who seems to be both one and the other, and it is only at the end that we can be certain of his true identity (the hero of the epic has no problem of identity for it is determined by a set of static disjuncts). *Stephen Hero's* participation in classic realism involves the text in the endless meanderings of the psychological novel. The text questions whether Stephen is really Maurice or Cranly or Cosgrave or some mysterious combination of these irreconcilable types. This psychological quest is abandoned in *A Portrait* where the other major characters, far from possessing some full identity, determine certain forms of address – practise a certain punctuation of Stephen's discourse. Lynch's punctuation is that of mechanical materialism: as Stephen discourses on his aesthetic theories, Lynch interrupts with comments about his poverty and they are both silenced by the passage of commerce:

> A long dray laden with old iron came round the corner of Sir Patrick Dun's hospital covering the end of Stephen's speech with the harsh roar of jangled and rattling metal. Lynch closed his ears and gave out oath after oath till the dray had passed (P 213).

Cranly spaces Stephen's words with constant references to femininity: he talks of a mother's love and it is during this final conversation of the book that a woman's singing interrupts the intellectual duel between them. Stephen acknowledges that Cranly felt 'the sufferings of women' (P 249).

I have attempted to emphasise the radical difference between the texts of *Stephen Hero* and *A Portrait*. At the same time it is necessary to insist that *A Portrait* is a contradictory work and that it articulates enough of the structure of classic realism to allow for its recuperation within the most traditional concerns.

Stephen's fantasy of himself as 'fosterchild' (P 101) holds out the constant promise of the production of a mythical father who will embody the name of Dedalus. This figure of the omnipotent father, who will fix an identity on his son, is in conflict with the text's deconstruction of the mechanisms of identification and this conflict runs through the text. In so far as the text refuses narrative and the father, it can investigate the world of the mother that lies buried in a patriarchal society, but in so far as the text figures an omnipotent father, in so far as it still tells a story then women will figure as bagatelles, mere means of exchange between men. This contradiction can be read in the descriptions of the woman that Davin meets on his way home from the hurling match. Her sexual advances threaten Davin's identity for they disrupt the position assigned to women by his nationalist ideology. But in so far as Stephen can understand her as a symbol for his artistic development she is reduced to a simple position, becomes an element within a male discourse. Indeed it is the discourse of the artist which, in its final position, threatens to assume the role of meta-language in the text. This position of finality is subverted, however, by the discontinuity of the five sections, each section is irreducible to the others because each uses a different discourse and there is no continuity of character and event to move us from one section to another. This is not to say that Stephen Dedalus does not remain the focus of attention, but in each section he is articulated differently and these articulations are not unified in a logic of progression. The discontinuity of time and language between each section makes it impossible for any one section to assume a primacy over the others.

The contradictory structure of *A Portrait* is the structure of perversion. The neurotic accepts that the sexes are different but he or she cannot admit that this disjunction is preceded by a moment of suspense. Sexuality can only be defined reciprocally: it is the possibility of difference that produces identity. The pervert, however, plays in the space of opening up and closing down this disjunction and endlessly deferring any final resolution. Thus the five episodes circulate by promising a conclusion that is never reached. It is this perversity that allows a minimal pleasure to be taken in the mother-tongue:

He closed his eyes, surrendering himself to her, body and mind, conscious of nothing in the world but the dark pressure of her softly parting lips. They pressed upon his brain as upon his lips as though they were the vehicle of a vague speech; and between them he felt an unknown and timid pressure, darker than the swoon of sin, softer than sound or odour (P 104).

There are endless discussions of *A Portrait* which turn around the attempts to find the position of the author in this 'authorless' work (cf. Booth 1961, pp. 323–336). All such attempts ignore the fact that the structure of the work allows for no such authorial stance and that the reader, to, is displaced from any position. The reader is constantly at *work* as discourse after discourse must be taken up without any fixed hierarchy to ensure the control and distance necessary to a position. If we wish to take this question of Joyce's position in the work seriously then perhaps Brecht provides the most appropriate and literal answer in his comments about his novel *The Business Deals of Mr Julius Caesar*:

My own activity seems to me to be of a wider range and more diverse than our theorists of realism believe. I feel myself to be very badly served by them. I am working at present on two novels, a play and a collection of poems. One of the novels is historical and requires extensive research in Roman history. Now the novel is the territory of our theorists. But I am not being malicious when I say that for my work on this novel: *The Business Deals of Mr Julius Caesar*, I have been unable to get any help from them. I can see no use for this accumulation of personal conflicts which the bourgeois novel of the last century borrowed from drama, for these long scenes, with painted backcloth and the evocation of interiors. For large sections I use the diary form. For other parts it has been necessary to change the 'point of view'. *As for my own personal point of view it appears in the montage of the two different points of view of the fictional narrators* (Brecht 1970, pp. 89–90). (The first 'point of view' appears in English in the original text; my emphasis.)

We can locate Joyce's position in the arrangement of discourses, in the montage. This, however, is not a position but an articulation, the articulation which is the 'I' at the end of the text. The 'I' of the closing diary is not a transparent position which can be reduced to a set of third person statements but a set of effects of language, the result of a montage of discourses. The end of the text is the guarantee of its beginning as the artist is produced who will write it. This guarantee is not that the enunciation of the text is possible from the end of the time of the enounced. It is that the enounced has been displayed as enunciation and at that point it is possible to compose a montage of the articulations that produce a body in language. In this montage there is no moment of dominance from which the reader's discourses are invited to a complacent and suppressed entry. It is this lack of dominance which enables us to locate the author – not as a simple source who, outside the text, can identify himself and then communicate this identity through a transparent discourse but rather as the play of possibilities produced by the various discourses of the text. The discourses in question are those of Catholicism and nationalism, of aesthetics and the artist, discourses which produce the 'I' that ends the text and immediately starts it again.

# 4
# A Radical Separation of the Elements: The Distanciation of the Reader in *Ulysses*

In the programme notes to *Mahagonny*, Brecht defines epic theatre as involving a radical separation of its elements and distinguishes three such elements in opera: the music, the text and the setting. He states his opposition to any integration of elements as follows:

> So long as the expression 'Gesantkunstwerk' (or 'integrated work of art') means that the integration is a muddle, so long as the arts are supposed to be 'fused' together, the various elements will all be equally degraded, and each will act as a mere 'feed' to the rest. The process of fusion extends to the spectator, who gets thrown into the melting pot too and becomes a passive (suffering) part of the total work of art. Witchcraft of this sort must of course be fought against. Whatever is intended to produce hypnosis, is likely to induce sordid intoxication, or creates fog, has got to be given up. (Brecht 1964, p. 37).

Brecht's objection to the 'integrated work of art' can best be understood as an objection to a naturalisation of the relationship between the signifier (the material image) and the signified (the meaning). It is possible, indeed in some sense inevitable, that the very distinction signifier/signified suggests an homology between material image and meaning. Saussure,

69

in the *Cours de linguistique générale*, introduced the concepts with the aid of this diagram:

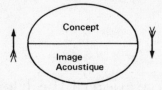

and all later diagrams are of a similar nature. Although Saussure emphasises that both signifier and signified are defined diacritically, the circle around them both suggests that there is some simple, indeed natural, relation between the two. Saussure's formulation of the sign's constitution makes it difficult to avoid a belief in a natural homology, no matter how much Saussure then insists on the arbitrary nature of the sign. Given this homology, it is doubtful if one can escape awarding a primacy to the signified; a primacy which finds its diagrammatic expression in the fact that the signified is placed above the signifier. Finally, and as a correlative of this dominance of the signified, there will be a tendency to ignore Saussure's strictures that signifier and signified are indissolubly entwined one with another (the famous image is the recto and verso of a piece of paper) and imagine an autonomous world of the signified. The possibility of such an autonomous world encourages a mistaken belief in the possibility for a subject (either collective or individual) of simple access to a unitary field of meaning. On this view, the signifier is a simple instrument of communication between two subjects, or two instances of the same collective subject, in either case both speakers bathe in the luxury of an evident logos.

The problem, in Saussure's work, is that there are two conflicting conceptions of language. Although both are opposed to the dominant comparative school of the time, they contradict each other at several points. Saussure's main purpose in the *Cours* is to found an object for linguistics – *la langue* – in which each element finds its definition through the differential structure (Saussure calls it a system) in which it is articulated. But

Saussure did not simply oppose system to representation. The systematic nature of language was elaborated in terms of a primacy of communication. This *primacy* of communication found itself, in turn, opposed to the comparativist view that communication was a *secondary* function of language. Although Saussure's belief in language as differential structure and his belief in language as communication are both in opposition to comparativist conceptions, they are at odds with one another.[1] It should not be thought, however, that there is any simple resolution to this problem. When Saussure found himself talking of language both as communication and as structure, it was not that he had failed to decide which had primacy but that he had touched on the constitutive contradiction of human subjectivity. If Saussure's own conception of the sign pulls language back to a simple homology and the subject to a full world of meaning, his radical insight into language as system denies the subject any such plenitude. Jacques Lacan has attempted to develop Saussure's insight while eradicating its psychologistic weakness, by recasting the diagram first proposed by Saussure into an algorithm of the form $\frac{S}{s}$:

Pour pointer l'émergence de la discipline linguistique, nous

[1] It is in the emphasis of one or other of these aspects of Saussure's thought that the dispute between the functionalists and the glossematicians takes place. The functionalists attempt to investigate the systematic organisation of the signifier through effects at the level of the signified. The only differences that matter are those that produce a change in meaning; those that alter the communicational charge of a particular linguistic unit. 'The phoneme can be defined satisfactorily neither on the basis of its psychological nature nor on the basis of its relation to the phonetic variants, but purely and solely on the basis of its *function* in language' (Trubetskoy 1969, p. 41; my emphasis); '*Une langue est un instrument de communication. . . .*' (Martinet 1973, p. 20). The problem with this approach is that the basic elements of the system have certain positive characteristics although these are defined oppositionally (thus the phonemes are described as voiced/voiceless etc.), rather than being of a strictly differential or formal character. Hjelmslev, rejecting such positive definitions as a misunderstanding of Saussure's radical insight that the object of linguistics is the form of the language (insight which finds its clearest expression in Saussure's chess metaphor), attempts a purely formal definition of a given language such that each element is simply defined by its relation of implication with other elements. See Hjelmslev, pp. 69–81.

dirons qu'elle tient, comme c'est le cas de toute science au sens moderne, dans le moment constituant d'un algorithme qui la fonde. Cet algorithme est le suivant:

$$\frac{S}{s}$$

qui se lit: signifiant sur signifié, le sur répondant à la barre qui en sépare les deux étapes. Le signe écrit ainsi, mérite d'être attribué à Ferdinand de Saussure, bien qu'il ne se réduise strictement à cette forme en aucun des nombreux schémas sous lesquels il apparaît dans l'impression des leçons diverses des trois cours des années 1906–1907, 1908–1909, 1910–1911, que la piété d'un groupe de ses disciples a réunies sous le titre de *Cours de linguistique générale*: publication primordiale à transmettre un enseignement digne de ce nom, c'est-à-dire qu'on ne peut arrêter que sur son propre mouvement. (To pinpoint the emergence of linguistic science we may say that, as in the case of all sciences in the modern sense, it is contained in the constitutive moment of an algorithm that is its foundation. This algorithm is the following:

$$\frac{S}{s}$$

which is read as: the signifier over the signified, 'over' corresponding to the bar separating the two stages. This sign should be attributed to Ferdinand de Saussure although it is not found in exactly this form in any of the numerous schemas, which none the less express it, to be found in the printed version of his lectures of the years 1906–7, 1908–9, and 1910–11, which the piety of a group of his disciples caused to be published under the title, *Cours de linguistique générale*, a work of prime importance for the transmission of a teaching worthy of the name, that is, that one can come to terms with only in its own terms.) (Lacan 1966, p. 497)

The importance of this reformulation can be summarised in three points. Firstly the primacy of the signified over the signifier is reversed, a reversal which is marked by the capitalisation of the signifier and the italicisation of the signified as well as by their change of place. Secondly the use of an algorithm suggests two different *levels* rather than Saussure's *faces* and this different terminology minimises the unity of the sign and emphasises its constitution from two heterogeneous areas. Thirdly this heterogeneity and the radical discontinuity between the two levels is emphasised both by the removal of the circle and the accentuation of the bar. For the bar can never be fully crossed and its resistance refuses to any sign the possibility of transparency, as the signifier constantly moves along its own differential chains.

The significance of Lacan's reading of Saussure is that there is now no possibility of the subject's full access to the world of meaning. Instead the subject is constantly caught and divided between two worlds (a division which is constitutive of them both). While at one level the conscious subject rests in the world of the signified, at a different level there is an *other* and dominant subject which races along the differential paths of the signifier and constantly disrupts the imaginary unity of the first. What is important is that Lacan's insight enables us to read in the organisation of language, the fundamentally divided order of subjectivity. The originality of Lacan's position is indicated by François Wahl in his comments on Lacan's analysis of Jakobson's thesis that language functions with the two basic tropes of metaphor and metonymy (metaphor producing the horizontal paradigmatic axis and metonymy the vertical syntagmatic axis):

Une chose est de repérer la métaphore comme loi d'organisation du discours, de la fonder comme un des deux pôles fonctionnels du language, de la retrouver dans les procès de condensation du mythe ou du rêve; une autre chose de lire, sous la substitution de signifiants qui fait la substance de la métaphore, un transport, une méta-phore *du sujet*: de reconnaître ainsi la place d'un sujet (du signifiant, c'est-à-dire de l'inconscient) excentrique à celui qui, sous les espèces du moi conscient, prétend parler; et d'en conclure qu'à se

poser toujours dans le fonctionnement indéfiniment substi-
tutif de la signifiance, le sujet ne peut être que toujours ail-
leurs, toujours avant. (It is one thing to pinpoint metaphor as
the organising law of discourse, to establish it as one of the
two functional poles of language and to find it at work in the
processes of condensation in myths or in dreams; it is quite
another thing to read, under the substitution of signifiers,
which is the substance of metaphor, a transport, a meta -
phor *of the subject*: to thus recognise the place of a subject (of
the signifier, that is to say, of the unconscious) excentric to he
who, in the colours of the conscious ego, claims to speak; and
to conclude from this that, by posing itself in the indefinitely
substitutive functioning of signification, the subject can only
always be elsewhere, only always ahead.) (Wahl 1968, pp.
393–4)

The subject, considered in these terms, is no longer a full
unity but a constant set of displacements inaugurated by a
primal (but never original) exclusion (castration) from a world
that was never full until it became empty; which emptiness we
continually attempt to fill. The political consequences of this
understanding are far-reaching. For it signals, in some sense,
the end of that idea of a full and self-sufficient individuality,
which has been dominant for so long in the West,[1] and heralds
in its place the ideal Brechtian crowd. Brecht's aim in his separation of the elements is to remove any possibility of an imaginary full individuality (such individuality is always conceived by
Brecht as the product of witchcraft or drugs) and to replace it
with the experience of self as a constant differentiation, a perpe-

---

[1] To date the rise and fall of such notions is hazardous work, possible only
after the most arduous empirical research and theoretical reflection. Suffice
then to *guess* that it is in the seventeenth century that one could locate the
mutation that gives birth both to the category of the subject and to that notion
of individuality. Cartesian philosophy, Newtonian physics and the grammar
of Port Royal all involve very precisely that notion of a unified and individual
subject of experience. It is the work of Locke which provides the most obvious
example of the need for a category of the subject in the justification both of the
new science and the new civil order of the bourgeoisie, an order already installed in England.

tual process of separation. This distance or separation is the gap between the full imaginary unity of a character and reality (which is indifferent to the character's fantasy of a rational progression in his life). It is the distance between the time of a life which appears to have its own logic (tragedy) and another, historical time which ignores that imaginary logic. And it is also the separation which occurs between the spectator who casts him or herself in the imaginary role of a theatre-goer and the indifference of the play to that role. To accomplish this last task (and it must be said that this task is essential to the accomplishment of the others, for the spectator must be de-centred too, lest he or she provide a centre for the play in his or her judging consciousness) the separation between signifier and signified must be accentuated so that the spectator is aware of the constant production of meaning in which he or she is implicated. To be conscious of our active involvement in meaning is to recognise the differences and contradictions which make of the individual a crowd. At the same time this recognition involves the recognition of how these differences and contradictions divide and unite us with our fellow spectators. The theatre-goer is thus constantly divided – constantly distanced – and this division is the fundamental awareness of *otherness*. It is with such an awareness that we leave the world of the imaginary for the real: 'La conscience accède au réel non par son développement interne, mais par la découverte radicale de *l'autre que soi*.' ('Consciousness does not accede to the real by its internal development but by the radical discovery of what is *other than itself*.') (Althusser 1965, p. 144)

This distance and division are conventionally hidden within classical theatre and are further occulted by various pressures in our society, a society concerned at all costs to establish an immutable human nature and a given reality. Jacques Derrida, in a series of brilliant and original works, has attempted to analyse the problem of the imaginary unity of the subject and meaning and to de-construct this full relation through an attention to writing. It is writing which, in the history of Western philosophy, has functioned as the emblem of drug, parasite, supplement, as a heterogeneity which is always *scandalous*. Derrida has insisted that in the immediacy of the spoken word we can ignore the fact that language is constituted as material difference and locate a moment in which truth will *present itself*. The precise form in which this truth is theorised, whether as Platonic *eidos*, Cartesian clear and distinct ideas, Russellian knowledge by acquaintance or whatever, is, in this context, unimportant. What these concepts share is a commitment to notions of correspondence and coherence which is menaced by writing, a fact which is recognised in philosophy by the distrust of the written word that Derrida demonstrates to be so general. Whereas in the spoken word we can pass to an interior, single source of meaning, the speaking subject, it is impossible to accomplish this interiorisation with the written word. For writing always runs out of itself towards an outside that surrounds and defines it, and it is only in terms of this outside that we can understand any sign. The individual letter gets its meaning from the letters and spaces that surround it and the book from the books and spaces that surround it. The emphasis is thus moved away from meaning as founded in a present and a presence, towards a conception of meaning as produced in the movement through time and space. But this conception of meaning entails that meaning is never finalised, it is always open to a fresh articulation. This threat to meaning is, of course, a threat to truth. For as the writing subject is fragmented into the play of differences constituted by the various discourses he or she is writing (and which depend for their meaning not on the individual subject but on their situation in time and space) so the presence, temporal and spatial, which is essential to the concept of truth is also fragmented into the play of differences. It is these differences which determine what objects will present themselves within a set of oppositions which are themselves always *already* constituted. It is in this perspective that we can grasp the force of Derrida's comment that 'Cette expérience de l'effacement du signifiant dans la voix n'est pas une illusion parmi d'autres – puisqu'elle est la condition de l'idée même de vérité . . .' ('This experience of the effacement of the signifier in the voice is not an illusion amongst others – for it is the condition of the very idea of truth. . .') (Derrida 1967a, p. 34)

The immediacy of the spoken word sustains dually the notions of presence and origin essential both to a conception of truth as independent and to a conception of language as representation. The twofold im-mediate nature can be characterised as follows:

(1) The spoken word as immediate founds a present which is marked by the unity of experience rather than by the movement of continual difference.

(2) The spoken word is experienced as im-mediate. That is to say that the medium of language (the vibrations which constitute the spoken word) is ignored as, in the existential situation, we perceive directly the presence of thoughts.

Language as representation and truth as presence are two sides of the same coin. The idea of language as non-productive is dependent on the idea that truth originates elsewhere (correspondence between world and mind) and is simply communicated by language. Thus in answer to the obsessive infantile question 'Where did thots come from?' (597.25) (where do the thoughts we have or the children (tots) we produce come from?) the experience of the spoken word offers explanations in terms of origins in a full presence. Thoughts originate in the presence of the subject to himself in self-consciousness, the child originates in the presence of the father at the moment of conception. Language represents the thought which exists independently of it and communicates this thought without interference; the mother represents the father and communicates his seed without interference in the son. But these answers are already infiltrated by a third term in the original question. 'Thots' also includes 'Thoth', the Egyptian god of writing, and with writing all such notions of representation are undermined. As writing runs ever outwards in that movement of exteriority already described, the meaning of a word, phrase or sentence is constantly being altered. Writing is thus represented in our own philosophical tradition (which Derrida analyses with such painstaking attention) as the very image of interference. It can only be represented as interference because of the prior assumption of some natural state of pure representation or communication. However, rather than interfering with some previously existent meanings, writing is, in fact, the producer of meaning. In an analogous fashion the mother can be thought of as the productive element (the activity of difference) which makes of the child not the copy of the father but the product of an activity.

It may be objected that this is 'heady stuff' or that it is impossible to 'export' such ideas across the Channel. But the distrust of writing as false and delusive in its materiality and the corresponding idea of the voice as a guarantor of the presence of consciousness to itself and thus the guarantor of truth is, and has been, central in England. To take merely one example of the crucial importance of this distinction between the spoken and written word in our cultural history, we can look at the concepts formulated by Leavis in the early 1930s concerning the idea of poetry as an imitation of speech. If, for example, one looks at an early article by Leavis on Milton one can find the opposition stated with perfect clarity. Leavis writes of a piece of Milton's verse that he admires:

> The texture of actual sounds, the run of vowels and consonants, with the variety of action and effort, rich in subtle analogical suggestion, demanded in pronouncing them, plays an essential part, though this is not to be analysed in abstraction from the meaning. The total effect is as if words as words withdrew themselves from the focus of our attention and we were directly aware of a tissue of feelings and perceptions (Leavis 1933b, pp. 127–8).

In this passage one can read the distrust of words which in their materiality prevent the experience of the author (life) shining through. Leavis continues by remarking that despite his talent as a poet, Milton abandoned speech in favour of a particular way of writing:

It became of course, habitual to him; but habituation could not sensitize a medium so cut off from speech – speech that belongs to the emotional and sensory texture of actual living and is in resonance with the nervous system; it could only confirm an impoverishment of sensibility (Leavis 1933b, p. 130).

The influential opposition between the Metaphysicals and Milton can be largely understood as an opposition between the truth of the voice and the falsity of writing. By an exemplary coincidence this article on Milton comes from the same issue of *Scrutiny* as that which contains the essay on 'James Joyce and the Revolution of the Word', in which Leavis dismisses Joyce's practices of writing as vicious and inorganic.

Writing menaces any simple notion of origin – any simple notion of an author – and with it the complementary notions of correspondence and coherence. In The Sirens episode in *Ulysses* the opposition between writing and the voice becomes the focus of the text's attention. As the material of language becomes the concern of the text, the reader can no longer pass through signifier to signified, can no longer bathe in the imaginary unity of a full self but must experience him or herself as divided, distanced, as *other*. The Sirens interrogates the distinction between the spoken and the written and this interrogation involves the deconstruction of any possible moment of origin offered by the figure of the father (or, indeed, of the author). This deconstruction has definite political effects as it demonstrates a contradiction between writing and nationalism.

The Sirens commences with 58 phrases of unequal length varying from the single word 'Listen!' (329) to the seven short sentences of 'Decoy. Soft word. But look! The bright stars fade. O rose! Notes chirruping answer. Castille. The morn is breaking.' (329) and the eleven phrases of 'Avowal. *Sonnez*. I could. Rebound of garter. Not leave thee. Smack. *La cloche*! Thigh smack. Avowal. Warm. Sweetheart, goodbye!' (329). Of these 58 phrases, 57 of them occur within the body of the text although they are often transformed and altered in their appearance. Thus the very first phrase 'Bronze by gold, heard the hoofirons, steelyringing Imperthnthn thnthnthn' (328) gets distributed through the first two pages of the continuous text. We find the 'Bronze by gold, Miss Douce's head by Miss Kennedy's head, over the crossblind of the Ormond bar heard the viceregal hoofs go by, ringing steel.' (331) but 'Imperthnthn thnthnthn' recurs a page later in 'Imperthnthn thnthnthn, bootsnout sniffed rudely, as he retreated as she threatened as he had come' (332), while the exact phrase 'heard the hoofirons, steelyringing' does not recur at all. Or, to take another example, the phrase 'A moonlight nightcall: far: far.' (329) recurs on pages 359–360 as 'Sour pipe removed he held a shield of hand beside his lips that cooed a moonlight nightcall, clear from anear, a call from afar, replying'. The 57th phrase of the opening sequence 'Done' (330) is the same word that closes the whole section.

What we can read in this passage is the interplay of letters and words as material. Far from attempting to efface the process by which meaning is produced, Joyce is concerned to show how the mechanism of writing works. The first two pages, in which phrases without a context litter the text, refuse all possible meaning. Deprived of a context which would allow us to read them (that is to say ignore them as signifiers in order to consume the signifieds that they communicate), the words become material objects which rest on the page and resist our attempts to subject them to meaning. Words without context cannot be read in terms of meaning because words derive their meaning, not from the fact that each word is charged with a definite thought, but from their position in regard to other words. It is the flow of whole sentences and paragraphs that allow us to pass over the word and ignore it in favour of meaning. A word is defined in terms of difference: the different letters that go to make it up, the different words that surround it, and this difference is a difference which is activated across time and space through reading.

The Sirens forces our attention on the activity of reading, which we can no longer claim is the consumption of a unity but must recognise as the constant movement of division. This section undertakes an investigation of writing as an activity in both time and space, for difference can only be produced *across* the page and *through* time. The spatial organisation of letters is what determines meaning but this spatial organisation is grasped in its particularity, as difference, through time and it is always in a deferred moment that the reader grasps the meaning of various signs. This deferred moment is at work throughout *Ulysses* as we constantly find phrases or words in new contexts which cause us to re-read their earlier occurrences. But The Sirens is that section in which the deferred moment is the major productive principle at work. After the 57 opening phrases we have the command 'Begin!' which institutes the process of writing and this process will be exaggerated throughout The Sirens. The repetition (our second reading) provides a large enough space of difference for the original phrases, and thus through time we can read their meaning. We cannot ignore the materiality of the letter because the words, no longer caught in a normal set of differences (which accord with our expectations and are thus ignored) are strange to us. This strangeness of the words is a strangeness of ourselves; they/we are no longer an evident source of meaning.

In this emphasis on the materiality of writing, Joyce's text breaks with a notion of internal thought or external reality outside a materially existent socially formed language. Thus the use of the Greek 'e', the difference of material inscription, marks the distinction between the text of Bloom and the text created by Bloom which is signed by Henry Flower. And as Bloom creates the character of Henry Flower so Joyce creates the character of Bloom, not in terms of creation and consciousness but in terms of production and language. Meaning is produced through a practice of writing, a process of differentiation of material signs. And as the Greek 'e' marks the different articulation of space so, in the text, this spatial organisation is grasped through time in a deferred moment:

'On. Know what I mean. No, change that ee' (360).

'You know now. In haste. Henry. Greek ee' (361).

There are many other instances where at macro-levels within the text the significance engendered by the material of words becomes a focus of attention. Two examples: on page 334 we read: 'Bloo whose dark eye to read Aaron Figatner's name. Why do I always think Figather? Gathering figs I think', and on page 346:

> – You did, averred Ben Dollard. I remember those tight trousers too. That was a brilliant idea, Bob.
> Father Cowley blushed to his brilliant purply lobes. He saved the situa. Tight trou. Brilliant ide.

In this second example, the words 'situation', 'trousers', and 'idea' are de-composed into material letters, but, in addition, the meaning of the word 'brilliant' is defined by what follows, by the difference that comes afterwards in a deferred moment. In Homer's *Odyssey*, the Sirens represent a pure voice which cannot be described by the text, for the text is implicated in the differential production of writing[1] Within Joyce's text, however, the Sirens episode does not function as an example of the power of the voice and the spoken word but undertakes the decomposition (in the musical sense of compose) of the voice and sound into the same play of material difference (play here considered in its mechanical sense, as the space in or through which a piece of mechanism can and does move) which constitutes writing. We have discussed the way in which the voice offers an experiential effacement of the material signifiers but it must be remembered that it is an effacement and not an abolition of this material. Marx was one of the first to emphasise the materiality of the spoken word when he wrote: 'From the start the "spirit" is affected with the curse of being "burdened" with matter, which here makes its appearance in the form of agitated layers of air, sounds, in short, of language' (Marx and Engels

[1] 'The Sirens are not described in the *Odyssey* although they sit 'in a meadow piled high with the mouldering skeletons of men, whose withered skin still hangs upon their bones'.

1965, p. 41). The Sirens can be read as the dramatisation of the materiality of language and it is Bloom as the writer in the drama who acts for the reader as the de-composer of the voice and music into material sounds. The voice is involved in the same play of difference through time and space that the text enacts in its practice of writing. Bloom, indeed, is identified as aiding the reading of this section when, in order to gain a pre-text for writing, he looks at the pages of the *Freeman*: 'Down the edge of his *Freeman* baton ranged Bloom's *your other eye*, scanning for where did I see that' (360; my emphasis). It is Bloom who is the reader's other eye and is, at the same time, his other I. By introducing writing, Bloom reads the voice for us but this read-ing introduces difference – introduces otherness – to the reader. Bloom locates the voice and music in material terms for the reader: 'The human voice, two tiny silky chords. Wonderful, more than all the others. That voice was a lamentation. Calmer now. It's in the silence you feel you hear. Vibrations. Now silent air' (357). Bloom de-composes the voice into the difference set up by the vibrations and their absence, the fundamental oppo-sition on which the voice is dependent. Similarly it is Bloom who recognises the importance of time (the deferred moment) in understanding sound:

Numbers it is. All music when you come to think. Two multiplied by two divided by half is twice one. Vibrations: chords those are. One plus two plus six is seven. Do anything you like with figures juggling. Always find out this equal to that, symmetry under a cemetery wall. He doesn't see my mourning. Callous: all for his own gut. Musemathematics. And you think you're listening to the ethereal. But suppose you said it like: Martha, seven times nine minus x is thirtyfive thousand. Fall quite flat. It's on account of the sounds it is.

Instance he's playing now. Improvising. Might be what you like till you hear the words. Want to listen sharp. Hard. Begin all right: then hear chords a bit off: feel lost a bit. In and out of sacks over barrels, through wirefences, obstacle race. Time makes the tune (359).

Bloom insists that music is a production of significance and not the magical result of a moment of creation. It is 'time that makes the tune' and Bloom repeats this insight later in the chapter when he thinks: 'Beauty of music you must hear twice' (367).

Bloom, however, is not the only indicator of the materiality of sound. Pat, the deaf waiter, stands as an example of a figure deprived of the experience of the effacement of the signifier in the voice. He 'seehears lipspeech' (365) and this dependence on vision entails an awareness of the voice as a production of a set of differences. (One might remark that it is exactly this 'seehearing' that is required for the 'soundscript' (219.29) of *Finnegans Wake*.) Symmetrically the blind piano-tuner depends on the different vibrations caused by his ubiquitous tapping stick and he must thus experience sound as material. But perhaps the most powerful image of the materiality of sound is the tuning-fork which rests in the centre of the Ormond Bar as a reminder to the reader of the vibrations that produce sound. It is interesting to note within this perspective that Joyce appears to have told Gilbert that the tuning-fork could be identified with Bloom.

Writing in The Sirens subverts any notion of a full presence in the act of reading through an attention to, and a drama-tisation of, the exteriority and the materiality of writing. In the same movement it dramatises the voice and sound (it is in this sense that we can understand the sequence as an 'imitation' of music) as the play of difference through time and space. This subversion destroys the possibility of the text representing some exterior reality and, equally, it refuses the text any origin in such a reality. The author does not create the meanings which are then conveyed by the text. For, as the meanings of the text are demonstrably produced by the distribution of the words through space and time, it is impossible to isolate the words of the text from the contemporary words surrounding it: the words of the reader. Despite appearances there is no definite limit to a book. The fact that we can read it involves a play of discourses which runs beyond the covers of the book and beyond any individual reader in the same moment. We cannot make the move to an author *outside* the text who produces meanings *inside* the text because we cannot locate the outside of the text; although we can distinguish its physical limits, we cannot 'close' the book. For if meanings are produced through the interplay of discourses then there is no outside to the text, there are no words which are not implicated in the play of the text. Thus is the text caught up in time and the movement of history. The attempt to move outside language and to find (found) the author as the creator of meanings is the attempt to fix meanings in an origin 'outside' the text. This attempt may often be desperate for if we cannot close the endless distance and difference opened up by the text then there is no longer any possibility of 'closing' ourselves. As the covers of the book dissolve, so we, too, lose our definite limits and the bodies of discourse which we are, become evidently open to a continuous re-articulation.

The image with which we can elaborate this radical concept of text is the shell which Miss Douce has bought back from the beach at Rostrevor and which adorns the shelf below the bar mirror 'where hock and claret glasses shimmered and in their midst a shell' (332). Those in the bar who listen to the shell and who are caught up in the experience of speech, locate the sound as present in the shell and originating in the sea. For us, however, guided by our *writer* Bloom, the sound is produced by the process of listening: 'The sea they think they hear. Singing. A roar. The blood is it. Souse in the ear sometimes. Well, it's a sea. Corpuscle islands' (363). Our ideas about what happens when we read a text are similar to the ideas of the drinkers about the shell. As we read a text we are convinced that the meanings we consume are present in the text and originate in the author. But just as the interaction of the shell and ear produce the roar that the drinkers hear, so it is the interaction between the discourses of the reader and the discourses of the text which produces the meanings that we extract. The sound is not present for the ear in the shell as the meanings are not present for the eye in the text. The sound is produced between the shell and the ear but this 'between' does not indicate a specific place 'between' the shell and the ear but rather the whole process produced 'between' (in the sense of together) the shell and the ear.

The sea which the hearers wish to locate outside the act of hearing is, in fact, within it; indeed, it is constituted by it. It is not the sea of Rostrevor they hear but the sea of their own blood. There is no beginning, no origin outside the act of representation and therefore the representational field is not constituted by a set of identities which are re-presented but by a play of differences in which each presence is defined metonymically by the absences that surround it. The lack of a simple beginning can be read in the text in the place of the command 'Begin'. This is the 58th phrase of the opening sequence and constitutes the beginning of the text we are reading, but the command is already caught up within the flow of signifiers and cannot be situated outside it. There is no outside to the text where meaning originates before language, rather the text's meanings are constantly being produced in the act of reading: in, that is, the juxtaposition of the discourses of the reader and the text.

The separation of the elements that Brecht demanded as the condition of an epic and political theatre was, above all, directed against any 'fusion'. It is, of course, at that moment in the text when Bloom submits to the singing – to the effacement of the signifier – that such a moment of fusion occurs. Caught up in the signified everyone merges into a single identity:

> The voice of Lionel returned, weaker but unwearied. It sang again to Richie Poldy Lydia Lidwell also sang to Pat open mouth ear waiting, to wait. How first he saw that form endearing, how sorrow seemed to part, how look, form, word charmed him Gould Lidwell, won Pat Bloom's heart (354).

It is this general fusion that provides the particular case of 'Siopold' (356). As everybody in the bar forgets difference to become a fictional unity (they are all Lionel), Leopold and Simon join together. It is with such a moment of identity that the interchangeability of pronouns is established: 'Come. Well sung. All clapped. She ought to. Come. To me, to him, to her, you too, me, us' (356).

It is also, of course, famously the moment of the illusion of fatherhood, the moment when the text finds an origin for itself as issued from the double loins of Leopold Bloom and Simon Dedalus. But, as with all such moments which are the products of the effacement of the signifier, the result is not simply unity but also, and necessarily, paralysis. This paralysis is produced in the Circe episode when the mirror (emblem of the efface- ment of the signifier) is the cause of a fusion between Stephen and Bloom. This imaginary union of the two is a paralysed Shakespeare and it is this same paralysis which grips those drinking and talking in the bar but which Bloom can escape through writing. It is as Bloom begins to write to Martha that he emphasises that every signifier produced threatens to reveal a different message from that entrusted to it. The world of writ- ing will demonstrate our subjectivity as constituted by division and difference (each new meaning subverts the unitary position of the subject) unlike the world of spoken communication where the apparent reception of our meaning by an-other ensures our own identity as we successfully identify with that other in the position of hearer. It is to the world of writing that the Sirens introduces the reader; we read the text as a 'letter selfpenned to one's other' (489.33/34). It is this world that Lacan indicates in his often repeated pronouncement that the speaking subject receives his or her own message from the other (the hearing subject) who returns it in inverted form.

The political effects of the recognition of this divided and dis- tanced subject are manifold. For Joyce, most specifically, it meant the refusal of the full unified identity offered by ultra- nationalism. As the drinkers listen in sentimental unity to the song of the Croppy Boy, Bloom considers Emmett's last words from the dock, those words which deny any possibility of writ- ing until the achievement of nationhood: 'When my country takes her place among Nations of the earth. Then and not till then let my epitaph be written. I have done.' Emmett's words spell out the paralysis of nationalism in its demand that writing must be stopped until the achievement of nationhood. But such a demand represses the only activity that can furnish a lasting liberation from the dominance of priest and king (priest and king being so many names for the signified). Bloom's response to Emmett's injunction is to fart. Bloom's anality introduces a *process of separation* which denies to the subject the *position of separated* from the world. In order to accede to the world of absence, the world of the sign, there must be instituted a division between the subject and the world. Such a division both relies on and represses the anal drive. Relies on, in so far as it is with anality that a distinction between inside and outside is established, represses, in so far as the anal drive constantly ruins that very distinction. The re-introduction of a process of separation corrodes both the identity of the subject and the transparency of the sign. As the subject dissolves so we leave the world of the sign and are confronted with the materiality of the signifier: the barrage of letters that are sprinkled through the closing lines of the section.

Emmett, and nationalism, wish to fix meanings and abolish writing. The last word of The Sirens is 'Done'. As part of the Emmett quote, the word has only one meaning, but within the text of The Sirens it gains the further meanings that the sequence has finished and that Bloom has farted. This fissuration of 'I have done' ensures that there is no final end to the text from which a one-to-one relation between signifier and signified can be imposed and this refusal of an ending is further emphasised by the fact that the 'Done' refers back to the command 'Begin'.

It was a common conceit at the end of the nineteenth century that music could be understood as the supreme expressive medium, as a perfect voice.[1] Underlying this idea was an ideo-

---

[1] Nietzsche provides a symptomatic example of the conflation between music and voice in this period. *The Birth of Tragedy* is written as a defence of Wagner, and Bernard Pautrat, in his book on Nietzsche, remarks that 'Durant toute cette période, la musique est pensée comme une sorte de *voix* ideale, mode d'expression éminent et premier par rapport auquel toutes les autres voix pourraient être jugées et évaluées.' ('Throughout this period, music is considered as a sort of ideal *voice*, the pre-eminent mode of expression

logy of the work of art as a vehicle for communicating a meaning from an origin (the artist) to a similarly discrete and unitary recipient (the aesthetic reader or listener). By insisting on the materiality of the vehicle (words or sounds), *Ulysses* transforms its relation both to its author and readers. An interesting parallel can be found in the contemporary efforts of the revolutionary composer Eisler and the revolutionary writer Brecht to alter the relation between art and audience. Walter Benjamin comments on their efforts as follows:

> In other words, the task consisted in the 'functional transformation' of the concert-hall form of music in a manner which had to meet two conditions: that of removing, first, the dichotomy of performer and audience and, secondly, that of technical method and content. On this point Eisler makes the following interesting observation: 'We should beware of over-estimating orchestral music and thinking of it as the only high art-form. Music without words acquired its great importance and its full development only under capitalism.' This suggests that the task of transforming concert music requires help from the word. Only such help can, as Eisler puts it, transform a concert into a political meeting. The fact that such a transformation may really represent a peak achievement of both musical and literary technique – this Brecht and Eisler have proved with their didaotic play *The Measures Taken* (Benjamin 1973a, p. 96).

This passage of Benjamin's is perhaps the best introduction we can have to reading The Sirens. For The Sirens makes of the

---

against which all other voices could be judged and evaluated.') (Pautrat 1971, p. 46) Nietzsche's texts also contain, however, another conception of writing which is in contradiction with the search for a pure mode of expression (cf. Pautrat pp. 48–122). Joyce himself would appear to have shared this belief in sound (music) as the true expressive medium in his youth: 'He read Blake and Rimbaud on the values of letters and even permuted and combined the five vowels to construct cries for primitive emotions' (SH 37), Later, however, he was to say that Rimbaud, although he had the artistic temperament, was 'hardly a *writer* at all' (letter to Stanislaus Joyce about 24 September 1905).

reader a Brechtian crowd, a crowd which is not a unity but a set of divisions which constitute opposing forces.

The Sirens dramatises the lack of a simple origin for a text – it deconstructs any possible author – and this dramatisation, deconstruction has immediate results. Deprived of the necessary interchangeability of pronouns, no dominant discourse can regulate and homogenise the heterogeneous discourses that are grouped under any one name in the text. With the end of an agreed 'it' of narration, there can be no more of those endless characters that the psychological novel is condemned to repeat and instead we can enjoy the contradictory interplay of language. The Cyclops sequence demonstrates this clearly, for the text works as a montage of discourses, without at any time offering us a final meta-language (an author's impersonal voice) which could control the riot of language which composes the text. The consequence of this riot is the lack of a standard by which we can judge the correspondence of these discourses to an exterior reality and the consequent experience of incoherence. Joyce describes the Cyclops section as proceeding 'explanatorily' (letter to Frank Budgen, 19 June 1919), but as one discourse takes up and explains another there is nothing for us to understand except the contours of language. The whole sequence works around a basic division between the narrative of the 'I' (the Nameless One) and the way this narrative is taken up and 'explained' by other discourses. But within this basic division there are further distinctions at work. Thus, within the discourse of the Nameless One, we can read the discourses of the Citizen and Bloom, not to mention a host of minor characters. The discourses of the counter-text are in no way uniform – varying from the legal (377–8) through the heroic (378–80 and continuously throughout the section), the spiritualist (389–90), the scientific (394), the academic (403–4), the parliamentary (409), the journalistic (412–14), the Elisabethan (436–7), the religious (440–2), and the biblical (449). Not that this list is in any way exhaustive, there are several passages which are extremely difficult to characterise, such as the marriage of Jean Wyse de Neaulan and Miss Fir Conifer (social-arboreal?) or the emuneration of the beauties real and symbolic of the Citizen's handkerchief.

To understand some of the devices at work within this section, let us look at the following passage which occurs on page 385:

> And lo, as they quaffed their cup of joy, a godlike messenger came swiftly in, radiant as the eye of heaven, a comely youth, and behind him there passed an elder of noble gait and countenance, bearing the sacred scrolls of law, and with him his lady wife, a dame of peerless lineage, fairest of her race.
>
> Little Alf Bergan popped in round the door and hid behind Barney's snug, squeezed up with the laughing, and who was sitting up there in the corner that I hadn't seen snoring drunk, blind to the world, only Bob Doran. I didn't know what was up and Alf kept making signs out of the door. And begob what was it only that bloody old pantaloon Denis Breen in his bath slippers with two bloody big books tucked under his oxter and the wife hotfoot after him, unfortunate wretched woman trotting like a poodle. I thought Alf would split.

In these passages we can read two descriptions of the same event. We can see this more clearly if we rewrite the text in the following fashion:

| 1st text | 2nd text |
|---|---|
| And lo, as they quaffed their cup of joy | (This takes up the Nameless One's preceding lines) |
| a messenger | Alf Bergan |
| godlike, radiant as the eye of heaven, a comely youth | little |
| came in | popped in |
| swiftly | round the door |

| and behind him | (in the second text this is expanded in the section from 'squeezed' to 'door') |
|---|---|
| and behind him | And begob what was it only |
| an elder | Denis Breen |
| of noble countenance | that bloody old pantaloon |
| of noble gait | in his bath slippers |
| bearing | with . . . tucked under his oxter |
| the sacred scrolls of law | two bloody big books |
| and with him his lady wife | and the wife hotfoot after him |
| a dame of peerless lineage | unfortunate wretched woman |
| fairest of her race | trotting like a poodle |

Ignoring for the moment that part of the second text which has no parallel in the first, what is important in this passage is not the truth or falsity of what is being said but how the same event articulated in two different discourses produces different representations (different truths). Behind 'an elder of noble gait and countenance' and 'that bloody old pantaloon Denis Breen in his bath slippers' we can discern no definite object. Rather each object can only be identified in a discourse which already exists and that identification is dependent on the possible distinctions available in the discourse. Therefore 'an elder of noble gait and countenance' can only mean something in relation to the other descriptions available within this heroic discourse. As 'that bloody old pantaloon' etc, is not one such description, it cannot be said to contradict it. Similarly 'that bloody old pantaloon' does not give us direct access to an object existing independently of a particular social world but again only means something within the whole system of the discourse, in relation to the other descriptions that it is not.

But there is more to say than this. For we recognise these representations as representations of the *same* event. But where can we obtain this identity except through some third discourse which identifies both as inadequate representations of an event which can be adequately represented within this third discourse? The third discourse is the reader's own and the reader is thus involved in the play of the text. But the method of this involvement calls in doubt the very notion of a final and adequate representation. Whereas a classic realist text always provides the third discourse to explain the other two (as, for example, in the scene between Mr Brooke and Dagley in *Middlemarch*) and thus offers the reader a method by which his discourses can innocently enter the text, Joyce's text contains no such point of entry. It is within this perspective that we can read the whole joyous activity of the Cyclops sequence, an activity which articulates in turn endlessly different ways of signifying the world but refuses to judge amongst them. This activity produces a certain lack of sense, a certain humour, which prevents us from ignoring the text in the name of some given order of reality. And as the object is thrown into the play of discourse so is the reading subject. For if the object is produced by the various positions and oppositions available within a given discourse, the positions that the 'I' can take up are equally limited. The ways in which the self can be identified and expressed in the discourse of the Nameless One and the heroic discourse of the counter-text are as different as the objects produced by these discourses.

It is the lack of a commanding position from which the reader can consume the discourses of the text that allows the Cyclops sequence to articulate the reader's own discourse on the same level as the other discourses of the text. Whereas the reader can enter the discourse of the realist text at an invited point (one could make a study of the interaction of the 'you' of the invitation at the beginning of so many nineteenth-century novels and the 'we' that replaces it) and then leave it at an indicated point after having consumed the content, the Cyclops sequence refuses this simple point of entry and exit. The realist text, in its assumption of a final language which effaces itself before an evident reality, leaves unquestioned, in a reciprocal movement, the reading subject. In the area outside inverted commas, in the absence of language, the reading subject can grasp its own organisation.

It is relevant to consider here the definition that Lacan gives of the written as opposed to the spoken word at the beginning of his essay 'L'Instance de la lettre dans l'inconscient:

> L'écrit se distingue en effet par une prévalence du *texte* au sens qu'on va voir prendre ici à ce facteur du discours – ce qui y permet ce resserrement qui à mon gré ne doit laisser au lec- tueur d'autre sortie que son entrée, que je préfère difficile. (Writing is distinguished by a prevalence of the *text* in the sense that this factor of discourse will assume in this essay, a factor that makes possible the type of tightening up that I like in order to leave the reader no other way out than the way in, which I prefer to be difficult.) (Lacan 1966, p. 493)

The difficulty of entry into a text is the lack of an agreed representational language – an agreed level of truth established on the equivalence of position between author and reader. The subject always takes its own discourses to be simply representa- tional and the lack of an agreed level where it can insert them will cause a difficulty which can be understood as laughter, fear or boredom. It is perhaps easiest to understand this trio of reac- tions by reference to the two experiential situations which re- produce some of the conditions of the subject before a *written* text. On the one hand the child listening to its parents' talk before it has finally mastered language and on the other the analysand listening to his or her own discourses come back to him or her punctuated by the silence of the analyst.

In the development of the child there is a moment when the infant (*infans* – unable to speak) learns a language. In this pro- cess of learning he or she becomes aware of certain places which he or she (as subject) can occupy and these are the points of in- sertion into language. Crucially this involves the learning of pronouns: the realisation that the 'you' the child uses to address the father or the mother can be permutated with an 'I' in a situation from which it is excluded, that is, when the parents speak to each other. In the same moment the child grasps that the 'you' with which he or she is addressed can be permutated with a 'he' or 'she'. This permutation reveals that the proper name is articulated within a constantly changing set of differences and that the child is only a signifier defined by a set of substitution relations. The binary 'I' – 'you' relation is transformed from two terms into a relational structure by the passage through the empty place of the 'he' or 'she', and it is through the experience of this empty place that the child learns language. The passage through this empty place is the necessary experience of exclusion which is essential to the proper control of language and the experience of this exclusion is the experience of death. It is this which gives discourse its fearsome quality because it involves, at the linguistic level, a castration, a narcissistic wound which must be submitted to if one is to accede to the adult world. As well as the experience of fear, however, the child can experience a discourse in which he or she is uncertain of his or her place as boredom (when the child gives up trying to understand) or as laughter (when the child takes as significant relations which are not allowed by the discourse). When the substitution rules have been mastered the child finds itself divided between two worlds: the world of the enunciation, where he or she is constantly in play as signifier, and the world of the enounced, where he or she is constantly in place.[1]

The classic realist text constantly tries to ignore the enunciation in order to fix a world of the enounced. Firmly established in their interchangeability, the text attempts to repress the pronouns as relations and assert them as absolute terms. It thus attempts to give itself an origin, outside the systematic and open substitutability of the reader's discourse, in a fixed and closed set of exchanges. The realist text generates itself by the same process of circulation through an empty term which we have identified in the child's mastery of language. This empty term is the 'it' of the narrative and the result of the passage through absence is that the realist text has the power to name, to construct fictions. The realist text, however, wishes to deny the absence on which it is constructed and to assert reality as

[1] Much of this argument is drawn from Luce Irigaray's article entitled 'Communications linguistique et spéculaire.' (Irigaray 1966).

the presence which provides the text with a simple origin outside language. To this end discourse must be divorced from the
narrative, enunciation from enounced; speech and language
can only figure as illusion.

Joyce's text in its emphasis on writing refuses the possibility
of any origin and therefore narrative falls back into discourse as
the text refuses to give us a fixed set of substitution rules. One of
the results of this loss of a masterful 'it', is that the text loses the
power to confer names. It is no accident that the story is told by
the Nameless One and that all of the characters appear pre-
dominantly as initials or as nicknames, rather than as *proper*
names.

It is the possibility of naming the object that characterises the
realist text and it is this same power that allows it to create a
character and donate a proper name. It is in the immediacy of
these objects and characters that we ignore the structure of language and take the subject as given. By ignoring language as
structure, the subject denies its own limits, but at the same time
accepts them. The subject is, at one and the same time, dominant in its 'presence' in the world and 'subjected' through the
already fixed positions allotted to it and its experience by the
structuring action of language. For as Jacques-Alain Miller has
put it, 'Structure is that which puts in place an experience for a
subject that it includes' (Miller 1968, p. 95). *Ulysses*, through its
refusal of any definite set of objects – and fixed identities – glories in its investigation of language as structure. The result of
this attention to structure is to displace the subject as the founding source of its world – a 'presence' – and thus to remove the
reader from his or her condition of subjection by allowing him
or her to take up many contradictory positions. It is this liberation of the subject from the condition of subjection that constitutes the burst of laughter that marks the joke and, if one
remembers Freud's comparison of the joke and the dream as
similar psychic products, then one could say that *Ulysses* is the
joke to *Finnegans Wake's* dream. The importance of this laughter
in *Ulysses* can be gauged by an attention to the laugh produced
by Stephen in the schoolroom sequence. The laugh is produced

by the riddle about the fox burying his grandmother. The structure of a riddle is another way of producing the uncertainty of
identities experienced in the Cyclops sequence. Stephen's reaction to the riddle is a burst of 'nervous laughter' (32) which in
its 'dismay' marks the extent to which he is still subjected:
'Secrets, silent, stony sit in the dark places of both our hearts:
secrets weary of their tyranny: tyrants willing to be dethroned'
(34). This dethroning (the liberation of the subject, the liberation of the signifier) is achieved for the reader in the text by a
deconstruction of any origin (any author) for the text which
could establish the text as a representation passing between
two identities. Thus the reader is cast unprepared into the text
(as the child before the parents' conversation) uncertain of
what position, if any, is to be allocated to him or her. Experience of fear, laughter and boredom.

The specific textual practices which produce this lack of
identity are too numerous to catalogue in detail, but in addition
to the simple juxtaposition of two descriptions of the same
event, one could notice the use of lists within the text. On page
424 we are informed by the Nameless One of the danger of Ireland being de-forested and Lenehan remarks 'Europe has its
eyes on you'. Starting from the double meaning of this phrase
(taken literally it can be understood to mean that Europe is
looking at Ireland's forests and whether England is ruining
them, and taken in the sense of the social cliché 'the eyes of the
world were on Hollywood tonight for the all star premiere . . .'
it can be read as meaning that Ireland's trees are at the centre of
Europe's social world), the text marries together two separate
sets of distinctions. The discourse of the forest and the discourse
of the society columns are joined together to produce the wed-
ding of 'the chevalier Jean Wyse de Neaulan, grand high chief
ranger of the Irish National Foresters, with Miss Fir Conifer of
Pine Valley'. In this whole passage with its extensive guest list,
a certain vocabulary which forms a very specific whole, that of
the forest and all the trees in it, is grafted onto the form of a
social column.

We can perhaps best grasp the 'shock' we feel on reading

Joyce's list of trees by contrasting it with how George Eliot employs the vocabulary of trees in the following passage:

> Brackenshaw Park, where the Archery Meeting was held, looked out from its gentle heights far over the neighbouring valley to the outlying eastern downs and the broad slow rise of cultivated country hanging like a vast curtain towards the west. The castle, which stood on the highest platform of the clustered hills, was built of rough-hewn limestone, full of lights and shadows made by the dark dust of lichens and the washings of the rain. Masses of beech and fir sheltered it on the north, and spread down here and there along the green slopes like flocks seeking the water which gleamed below (George Eliot 1880, vol. 1, pp. 144–5).

In this passage 'beech and fir' are part of an extensive list and this list functions, in its catalogue of obvious identities, as a guarantee of an evident external reality which is being revealed in the book and exists independently of the book's written existence. The activity of writing as the production of a set of meanings is effaced and writing becomes a simple representation, the rendering of identities existing independently of language. 'Beech and fir' in their solid particularity guarantee the neutrality and transparency of the writing. Joyce's list functions in almost exactly the opposite manner. First of all its completeness (it includes all the trees) ruins the particularity of the identities. 'Beech and fir' work through the exclusion of other possibilities, but in Joyce's text there are no possibilities which are excluded and with this overload of sense we fall into nonsense. Instead of the identities shining through and effacing the writing, the progressive adding of more and more identities achieves the opposite effect. Our attention is directed to the way in which writing is acting as a producer of meaning rather than as a picture of an unconstituted reality. Representation gives way to production.

But Joyce's text draws attention to its activity as a producer of sense in a second way. For the content of the list (the trees) is enumerated within a different form (the society column). This transposition of languages, this confusion of form and content, renders the words on the page opaque. They can no longer function as a transparent window on the world. In *Ulysses* language ceases to be a passage between two moments of full presence (the object and consciousness) but insists on its reality which exists prior to any individual subjectivity or object. As *Finnegans Wake* puts it: 'But the world, mind, is, was and will be writing its own wrunes for ever, man, on all matters that fall under the ban of our infrarational senses,' (19.35/20.1).

The divisions that we can create in language are always *already* made, as are the positions that can be taken up by the subject. And it is with this fact in mind that we can consider the practice of listing which is constant throughout the Cyclops. To list is to apply a set of identities to the world and it is the power of language to produce lists, to articulate a set of divisions, which is the power to produce a world for the senses. The lists within the text are all, in some sense, ruined; deprived of their ability to disappear and reveal the world. Instead, it is writing which dominates the scene. The continuous setting up of differences, the endless production of identities and sense – it is this which constitutes the text of the Cyclops. It is worthwhile, given this argument, to look back at the original version of the Cyclops which was published in *The Little Review* of November 1919 and March 1920. Practically every list that appears in *The Little Review* text is expanded for the final book publication. A good example of this process is the transformation of the Irish heroes that are engraved on the seastones which hung from the Citizen's girdle. In the original version the list preserves the opposition Irish and non-Irish: 'Cuchulin, Conn of hundred battles, Niall of nine hostages, Brian of Kincara, the Ardri Malachi, Art MacMurragh, Shane O'Neill, Father John Murphy, Own Roe, Patrick Sarsfield, Red Hugh O'Donnell, Dom. Philip O'Sullivan Beare.' When we get to the final version the list has increased to nearly one hundred names and its ability to function as a list is ruined by the inclusion of 'Patrick W. Shakespeare', 'Goliath', 'Herodotus' among numerous others (383). This ruination of the immediacy of the object allows, in the appearance of language as structure, the liberation of the reading subject from the positions in which it is subjected in its own discourses. I have already talked of the way in which *Ulysses* is no longer concerned with representation but with montage, and it should now be clear that montage involves, as the essential *motor* component of its effects, the discourse of the reader.

This dynamic effect of the reader's discourse can be understood in terms of the lack of a prescribed entry to the text, and I have attempted to demonstrate the lack of such an entry in Cyclops. However, it can also be explained in terms of the concomitant lack of an exit from the text, the lack of a moment of closure in which the various discourses of the text are ordered in terms of the narrative's dominance. This lack of closure is obvious in the story told by the Nameless One. Throughout his narrative there are two central discourses, two rival areas of representation and meaning. We are offered to choose between the language of the Nameless One which identifies everything in terms of malicious motives and hypocritical actions and the language of the Citizen which identifies everything in terms of Ireland. There is a certain expectation that either the text will provide a meta-narrative which will correct these two discourses or that Bloom (our hero) will explain and reveal the mistakes that the Citizen and the Nameless One are making and that this explanation will demonstrate the true nature of things.

Any hope of a meta-narrative is constantly destroyed by the counter-text which, far from setting up a position of judgement for the reader, merely proliferates the languages available. As if to emphasise the lack of a position of judgement, the mutual subversion of discourses is carried over from the paragraph to the sentence in the final moments of the section. At the very end of the sequence the language of the Nameless One and the prophetic language of the explanatory text are placed side by side in the same sentence: 'And he answered with a main cry: *Abba! Adonai!* And they beheld Him even Him, ben Bloom Elijah, amid clouds of angels ascend to the glory of the brightness at an angle of fortyfive degrees over Donohoe's in Little Green Street like a shot off a shovel' (449). No discourse within the text is even allowed the privilege of physically ending it. This juxtaposition offers us no definition of the discourses within the text but throws us back to the ceaseless interplay of relations which is produced by the reader's discourse acting on the text.

But if the narrative refuses to produce a position against which the other discourses can be read off (and this because the narrative itself has revealed itself as discourse), our hero Leopold might be expected to do the job. But Bloom's discourses, as related by the Nameless One, reproduce the montage of discourses within the whole sequence. For Bloom, unlike the Citizen and the Nameless One, is not fixed within one discourse but participates pleasurably in several. Thus, in the brief time he is in the pub, he enters into the discourses of science (394) and law (405) as well as those of Irish nationalism (410) and human compassion (416). Bloom's entry into the play of languages means that he cannot erect a fixed representation of the world which will explain the other languages. When asked to define what life really is he comes out with: 'Love, says Bloom. I mean the opposite of hatred. I must go now . . .' (432). Bloom refuses to stay to define the identity of life, to represent and to fix it. What is opposed to the violence of the citizen (based as it is on a fixed representation of the world) and the verbal violence of the Nameless One (also founded in a fixity of meaning) is the joyful entering into the various ways of signifying world and self. This is both Bloom's activity in the text and the activity of the reader in reading the text.

The insistence on a dominant discourse can be linked specifically to violence. The Citizen's violence in the text arises from the misunderstanding of Bloom's remark to Bantam Lyons that he was just going to throw his newspaper away. This remark can only be given one interpretation, one identity, by the betting fraternity of Dublin. It can only be represented in one way and it is this fixed interpretation that leads to violence. The Cyclops section is that part of *Ulysses* which is concerned with the eye and with sight. What we recognise as we read through the juxtaposition of various discourses is that the world we see is determined by the discourses we speak. Our senses and our sense are one. If we return to the passage already discussed when Denis Breen passes the pub, it demonstrates that there are some actions (Bob Doran asleep in the snug and Alf Bergan laughing at him) which cannot be represented within the heroic language; they are invisible. But there is no discourse which sees everything, no discourse which will epiphanise the world in some total moment. Furthermore it is action based on this illusion of a final fixed reality which is allied in the Cyclops (as elsewhere in *Ulysses*) with violence and intolerance.

The contrast between the Citizen's use of lists and parodies and the use of lists and parodies within the 'counter-text' can illuminate the links between the fixation of subject and object in a world of meaning and the eruption of violence. The Citizen reads out one list and one parody (384–5 and 434–5). But both the list and the parody are immediately contained within the fixed area of representation which constitutes the Citizen's world. The list of births, marriages and deaths in the *Irish Independent* represents only the English domination of Ireland. And the parody of the Zulu chief's visit to England in the *United Irishman* is completely contained within an anti-colonialist ideology. Bloom threatens the area of the Citizen's representation because he cannot be identified. Is he a Jew or an Irishman? And it is this difficulty of identity that produces violence for, in the threat to the Citizen's area of representation, Bloom poses a threat to the Citizen himself. If the object disappears then, in a reciprocal movement, the subject is displaced. The struggle against this displacement is the very root of violence.

The nature of the reader's involvement with the text renders his or her own discourses plural. Deprived of a unitary position of dominance, the reader's discourses distance themselves one from the other as they declare their contradictions. The distance thus opened provides the space for new things to be said. These methods of subverting the reading subject suggest that Joyce's texts can be considered as the novelistic equivalent of a

Brechtian drama. It is interesting that, independently, both of them turned to the term 'epic' to describe their work. Not that epic should primarily be understood as a positive term. In fact it functions as a negative moment in a constant struggle against classic realism and narrative. The text must subvert any promise of origin in an author, coherence in itself, or correspondence with a given reality, in order to engage with the subject in a distancing from any final identification. It is in this perspective that we can understand the relative lack of interest generated by *Exiles* or Joyce's poetry. In them there is an insufficient separation of the elements and the result is that the promise of an original message envisioned by the author is all too insistent. One can, however, indulge for a moment in fantasy – *Exiles* produced by Brecht while in Denmark in 1938, in exile and working on novels – that indeed might have been interesting.

# 5

# City of Words, Streets of Dreams: The Voyage of *Ulysses*

*Ulysses* is a voyage through meaning: a voyage through all the discourses available in English in 1904. As Bloom and Stephen move through Dublin so the writing moves through the city of words that is English. And in this attention to discourses it is not simply the reality represented by language that is in question but the desire that speaks through language. In the analysis of George Eliot's texts it was indicated how the appeal to a final meta-language involved the denial of the existence of desire in the affirmation of a full presence for both subject and object. It was suggested that one could read against the meta-language of these neurotic texts and that the process of reading was thus transformed into an active operation by the reader in which the reader's discourses and those of the text could meet to produce new discourses in which the subject's place was no longer assured.

In Joyce's texts this work of disruption is already accomplished for the reader and, in the attention paid to the materiality of language, we find both the fragmentation of a fixed reality and the possibility of desire 'speaking' through this fragmentation. But what is desire? Desire can be defined (after Lacan) in terms of the subject's relation to language. If we distinguish between *need*, which can be satisfied by an object (thus hunger is satisfied by food) and *demand*, which is addressed to another (in order to obtain the object I must enter into the world of language and inter-subjectivity) then we can understand *desire* as the product of the entry into language in so far as that entry involves relations over and above any particular sets of demands. Language institutes a space (available for fantasy) in which the subject can never grasp its own constitution:

> Il n'y a pas un inconscient parce qu'il y aurait un désir inconscient, obtus, lourd, caliban, voire animal, désir inconscient levé des profondeurs qui serait primitif et aurait à s'élever au niveau supérieur du conscient. Bien au contraire, il y a un désir parce qu'il y a de l'inconscient c'est-à-dire du langage qui échappe au sujet dans sa structure et ses effets et qu'il y a toujours au niveau du langage quelque chose qui est au-delà de la conscience et c'est là que peut se situer la fonction du désir. (There is not an unconscious because of some unconscious desire, obtuse, heavy, Caliban-like, even animal-like, an unconscious desire raised up from the depths, primitive and having to bring itself up to a higher level of consciousness. Completely on the contrary, there is desire because there is unconsciousness, that is to say language which escapes the subject in its structure and its effects, and because there is always at the level of language something which is beyond consciousness and it is there that one can situate the function of desire.) (Lacan, quoted in Safouan 1968, pp. 252–3)

This definition can be further articulated in terms of a logic of separation. We are long familiar with those three stages (the oral, the anal and the phallic) which are used to characterise the small infant's development. What is essential to understand is that each of these stages turns around a separation (from the breast, the faeces, the phallus) and it is these separations which allow language and desire to function. We can understand the nexus of relations which constitutes language, the other and the object by considering the small infant in the first stage of its development. We can postulate the child as experiencing two initial states of being: one of satisfaction at the breast and one of dissatisfaction which finds animal expression in the cry. It is in the moment when the infant correlates the cry with the experience of dissatisfaction and its abolition (a sufficient volume of crying will summon the mother) that the cry ceases to be a signal and becomes a sign. That is to say that the crying is no longer simply linked to the experience of dissatisfaction as effect to cause but now has a meaning which can be defined diacritically with the possibility of not crying. But this account demonstrates how the correlation of the cry with the experience of dissatisfaction and its abolition is indistinguishable from the identification of the breast as object and, further, as an object in control of another. To identify the breast as an object is to recognise the possibility of its absence when it is present, to recognise in the moment of satisfaction the possibility of dissatisfaction. An object can only be defined as a perpetual play of presence and absence and it is with this play that we enter into the world of desire. Desire must not be confused with the pleasure of union with the breast (the state of satisfaction and a minimum of tension) but is the recognition of an object which can bring about the abolition of dissatisfaction. But in so far as the recognition of an object involves that object's absence, it can never be fully enjoyed. For even at the moment of the abolition of need, at the moment when the object is present, its absence will be inscribed as a possibility. Desire is thus constantly in search of a perpetually lost object. It is with this search that we find counterposed to the pleasure of a constant minimum of tension, the desire for the maximum of tension and its discharge in a never-ending chain. The setting up of the world of communication – of demand – is also the setting up of an unconscious – of desire. Desire is that which rests over and above any demand and which is indeed, to use Lacan's term, completely 'excentric' to consciousness. Desire is not centred like demand in the needs of the subject. Indeed it is not centred at all, but occurs as the movement along the chain of differences that constitute the recognition and abolition of need through the world of demand.

The representational text, or rather, the text that offers itself as representational, attempts to elide the virtuality of language and desire and to allow reality to appear as a full presence uncontaminated by the implication of absence. As communication between two subjects, writer and reader, the text attempts to treat language as pure transparency. Outside the constitutive process of separation it wishes to treat language and reality as separate. It is in so far as this process of separation makes itself felt (as anxiety) that the text is neurotic. It is in so far as separation has been denied successfully that the text can glory in its own self-possession; in its undoubted command of a founding consciousness. This self-possession (as we shall see) is predicated on the possession of the power of the phallus, a possession conferred by a radical miscognition of sexual difference and language. Buck Mulligan, as his nickname implies, stands for a phallic world that can ignore the possibility of difference because it is confident of its unchallengeable possession of the phallus. His phallic smile, 'his white glittering teeth' (5), contrasts with Stephen's mouthful of rotting teeth, a contrast Mulligan insists on when he dubs Stephen 'Toothless Kinch' (27). The realm of the Buck is also marked as the realm of communication, not only implicitly by his easy rhyming poetry and facile conversation but explicitly when the text identifies him with Mercury, the god of communication (23).

Stephen, however, cannot accede to this realm because he is still tied to the mother and has yet to find a way to sever those ties. If separation is the key term in the functioning of language and desire, the separations from the partial objects of infancy only find themselves articulated in the more general separation from, and renunciation of, the mother. It is this renunciation which Stephen is unable to make. For Freud, the separation from the mother is an essential moment in the structure of the Oedipus complex, a structure through which all human animals must pass in their transformation into men and women.[1]

[1] Although Freud originally postulated a simple reversal of the Oedipus complex for women, later in his life he saw that attachment to and separation from the mother was perhaps the most important factor in the development of the female psyche as well. This chapter, as *Ulysses* demands, is devoted to the male infant's relation to the mother. The relation between daughter and

If, in the first instance, the male child, in his position of dependence, constantly asks himself why he is loved by the mother, then it is also at this stage that he constantly attempts to fit himself to her desires. In so far as her desire is unconscious, this attempt to retain the mother's love will take the form of an endeavour to mould himself to what she asks him to be. In other words, the child's concern is to conform to her demand. The recognition of sexual difference offers a solution to the riddle that has perplexed the child from birth: he is loved because he is the phallus that the mother lacks. This fact explains her affection. But simultaneously, in a logically distinct moment, he recognises that the mother's desires are organised in terms of the father who is understood as a rival phallus. If the mother is now understood to be fundamentally lacking in her being (thus her love for the child and the father), the father is understood as a full presence. As the father is without lack (he is the phallus incarnate), he functions as the cause of his own desire. The element of hate enters when the child realises, in a third stage, that the father is also articulated within an organisation of desire that he does not control. The father is not the full presence that he promised to be; he, too, is lacking in his being. Popular accounts that the child sees himself as the rival of the father reduce the significant features of the third stage of the Oedipus complex. For in so far as the father is a rival, they are both endowed with the phallus. The child's hatred of the father (which Freud understood as the most deeply buried and the most firmly entrenched emotion in men) is provoked by the father's failure to fill the role assigned to him by the child: to be the cause of his own desire. It is at this third and final stage, when the child admits that he can never become omnipotent, that he submits to a symbolic castration which brings the Oedipus complex to a close. This submission involves the introjection of an image of the self which admits the lack in being that constitutes us as speaking and desiring animals. This third stage, however, remains for us, caught in a

_____

mother becomes important in *Finnegans Wake* and will be discussed in the next chapter.

patriarchal society, only a partially realised possibility. All the efforts of society are devoted to encouraging as complete a regression to the second stage as is conformable with sanity. The fullest realisation of what it might be to finish with the Oedipus complex and allow ourselves to experience the workings of language and desire is to be found in the texts of those writers and thinkers who mark the end of our era, characterised by Derrida as phallogocentric, but who accomplish this task at the risk of psychosis. *Ulysses* is pre-eminent amongst those untimely works available to us in English, and the risk involved in writing it was recognised by Joyce in his statement to Jacques Mercanton that 'it was a terrible risk that book. A transparent sheet of paper separates it from madness' (Mercanton 1967, p. 46). To understand how *Ulysses* participates in this third stage of the Oedipus, it is necessary to examine the mechanisms at work in the earlier stages.

We can sketch the construction of the phallus by considering that moment of startling significance in the life of a young boy (a moment to whose importance the whole of psycho-analysis testifies) when he recognises that a woman does not have a penis. In order to grasp the fact of absence, the child must contrast it with the presence of his own penis. But so to do is to admit the possibility of that penis's absence. This interplay of presence and absence turns the penis into a signifier, the signifier of sexual difference. To distinguish between the physical object which the little boy possesses and the signifier, which by its very nature can never be possessed, Lacan reserves the term 'phallus' to designate the signifier. It is the small boy's unwillingness to admit the possibility of the absence of his own penis that leads him to deny the reality of the phallus as signifier. This is the second stage of the Oedipus in which the child attempts to *be* the phallus that the mother lacks in that neurotic condition whose very existence bears witness to the facts it endeavours to deny. Representation enacts the same structure in its efforts to fix a signifier for the subject in a perpetual signified.

However, it is only through the admission of lack, the acceptance of the signifier, that desire can function. In a world of presence there is no absent object to be desired. The strategy which contains the admission of lack within an area of control (and thus preserves the inviolability of the penis together with a minimal access to desire) is that adopted by the fetishist. The fetishist inaugurates desire by the *replacement* of the mother's penis. This *replacement* involves an admission of the absence of the mother's penis (hence the need for a replacement) and yet an assertion of its presence in the substitute. The generality of the structure of fetishism in our society was hinted at by Freud in his essay on that subject when he stated that the prototype of the fetish was the man's own penis. In that essay Freud locates the construction of the fetish in the moment when the small boy sees that the mother does not possess a penis but he introduces a comparison which suggests other possibilities:

> What happened, therefore, was that the boy refused to take cognizance of the fact of his having perceived that a woman does not possess a penis. No, that could not be true: for if a woman had been castrated, then his own possession of a penis was in danger; and against that there rose in rebellion the portion of his narcissism which Nature has, as a precaution, attached to that particular organ. In later life a grown man may perhaps experience a similar panic when the cry goes up that *Throne and Altar are in danger*, and similar illogical consequences will ensue (Freud 1927e, *21*: 153).

This final sentence would seem to suggest that the forms of masculine authority become invested as a guarantee of the man's possession of the phallus, that is to say as cause of his own desire. If the famous 'objects' of fetishists are the product of a single traumatic moment, the transformation of the man's own penis into a fetish involves the designation of objects and institutions with phallic authority in the face of the evident failure of the real father.

If we now return to our characterisation of the setting up of the world of communication and the unconscious, of demand and desire, we can make some attempt to delineate the various relations of the speaking subject to language in terms of the Oedipus complex. The neurotic, in his attempt to deny the existence of the mother's desire, threatens to abolish the world of demand. For because her desire is opaque (it is its very opacity which terrifies), the neurotic endlessly waits for the mother's demand which will finally ask him to be what she lacks and thus end her intolerable situation. But such a demand is impossible for demand is always determined by what it is not, by absence and lack. It is finally language that the neurotic represses and it can be said that the neurotic is always speechless (the job of the analyst is to furnish the patient, from the patient's own discourses, with the material for his desire to speak). The fetishist's world is the world of communication where because desire is under control (the imaginary possession of the phallus confers an imaginary control), the differential nature of demand can be ignored. Language is reduced to a pure meeting of minds, although it might be added that those minds must all have bodies similarly endowed: women, of course, are rigorously excluded from this world. This is made clear in the opening chapter of *Ulysses* where the milk woman cannot understand Mulligan's intellectual speech nor Haines's Irish. The necessity of the exclusion of women for the possibility of that intellectual communication where minds meet can be read in Eryximachus' decision at the opening of the *Symposium*:

> Since, then, we have come to this decision, that each man shall drink merely as much as he chooses, and that there shall be no compulsion, I propose in addition that we should send away the flute-girl who has just come in – let her play to herself or, if she likes, to the women of the household – and entertain ourselves today with conversation (*Symposium* 176e).

But if the fetishist must ignore the reality of women to bathe in the luxury of communication (and Plato's dialogues reveal the centrality of that ignorance in the genesis of Western thought), the pervert, in his recognition of the reality of women, is condemned to submit to a circulation of signifiers, fantasy, in which his position is never assured and in which he experiences language as system. In so far as from this experience he can find a place of rest, he will rejoin the world of communication; in so far as he fails, he will sink beneath the waves of psychosis. The psychotic suffers not from a neurotic fixation in the signified but from the uncontrollable play of the signifier.

Stephen, in the opening of the book, is trapped within the speechless world of the neurotic. While on the one hand he wishes to accede to the male world of communication, he is unable to, except under the influence of drink. 'The sacred pint alone can unbind the tongue of Dedalus' (21), says Mulligan, and throughout *Ulysses* drink provides access to a male community and verbal communication. It is the mother who lies as a barrier across Stephen's entry to this world. In so far as Stephen feels himself the subject of his mother's desire he cannot believe in the father as self-sufficient cause of desire. The father's inability to function as a rival leaves Stephen snared in the second stage of the Oedipus, desperately denying the existence of lack and thus of desire. Only by undertaking the voyage of writing can he produce the space in which his desire could speak; that desire of which he knows nothing. The opening of the book finds him still struggling to be that full presence that constitutes neurosis. On the beach he talks of 'signatures of all things I am here to read, seaspawn and seawrack, the nearing tide, that rusty boot' (45), and the whole of the opening three chapters are a process of reading the signatures from the history lessons, the mathematical symbols, and Mr Deasy's letter about foot and mouth disease. The signatures, however, are conceived as presenting some full meaning which his full 'I' can decipher. But it is exactly this full 'I' which can know nothing of language: of the experience of lack and difference. Thus the poem that Stephen writes on the beach is invisible. For within this section writing exists only as repressed possibility: an insistence on materiality and difference, absence and lack, which, in its return, will disrupt the clear subjectivity of this section and make language and desire possible.

If the reader can position him or herself securely in this

opening section (he can identify with Stephen's discourse), that dominance is soon undermined as the voyage of writing gets under way. The first displacement is the change from Stephen to Bloom. Bloom also spends the majority of his introductory chapters engaged in the act of reading. The advertisements for the farm at Kinnereth, Milly's letter, Matcham's masterstroke, Ruby: the pride of the Ring, the Plumtree advertisement, the multicoloured hoardings, Martha's letter – the list is very long. What is significant for our purposes is that the reading is, as it were, a reading at double remove: we are placed in the situation of reading through reading. This fact is brought to our attention with the move from Stephen to Bloom. If one set of discourses allows us to settle ourselves in a fixed position, two reveal system rather than position, discourse rather than subject.

This displacement is accelerated in the newspaper office when our two introductions to the text (Stephen and Bloom) cross each other's paths. What are important in this juxtaposition (which is a juxtaposition of discourse rather than character) are those phenomena of repetition which are crucial within the text of Ulysses and which constantly insist on the nature of the text as written, that is to say as a set of traces that can be constantly reworked. In the opening six episodes there are many instances of repetition. For example, Bloom reads the letter from Milly twice, once briefly (75) and once at length (79–80). The repetitions within these opening chapters retain the same significant oppositions as the original occurrences, the same discourse prevails. Although Milly's letter is expanded, this expansion does not alter the position inscribed for the reader. If we turn to the Aeolus section we find that the repetition in question is of a different order:

SOPHIST WALLOPS HAUGHTY HELEN SQUARE ON
PROBOSCIS. SPARTANS GNASH MOLARS. ITHACANS
VOW PEN IS CHAMP

– You remind me of Antisthenes, the professor said, a disciple of Gorgias, the sophist. It is said of him that none could tell if he were bitterer against others or against himself. He was the son of a noble and a bondwoman. And he wrote a book in which he took away the palm of beauty from Argive Helen and handed it to poor Penelope.

Poor Penelope. Penelope Rich.

They made ready to cross O'Connell Street (188).

In this passage the repetition brings something new into play. If we investigate the constitution of this novelty more closely, we can perhaps understand the strategies which prevent the subject assuming a position of dominance with regard to his discourses. The confident 'I' of communication – the analogue of phallic security – disappears to allow something else to speak. This something else is discourse out of control of a subject; desire which in its radical otherness strikes at the heart of our narcissistic constitution. The original newspaper headline is written within one set of significant oppositions (those of popular journalism) and repeated in another (those of classical scholarship). The phenomenon recalls those practices analysed in the Cyclops section and they produce the same effect: the subject can no longer take up a founding position outside his or her own discourses but is articulated within them. It is in the newspaper office that the reading subject is first prevented from occupying a fixed place and is plunged into a juxtaposition of discourses. And this interplay of discourses *is* the activity of the writing of the text. The act of writing is no longer hidden in the copying down of an already written (reality) but has become the active investigation of the subject's positionality. As the activity of writing thus insists within the text, the poem that Stephen wrote on the beach can make its appearance (168).

In the Aeolus chapter, the text no longer provides a centre for itself. If, in the first six chapters, Bloom's or Stephen's consciousness could be taken as central, this is no longer the case in the newspaper office. This change is obvious in those pages when J. J. O'Molloy is relating the speech made by Seymour Bushe in the Childs murder case. His speech is punctuated by

Stephen's thoughts and the other events taking place in the office. Many of these events are not linked to Stephen's consciousness and seem to be retailed by an 'impersonal narrator', although such a description, which implies a centre for the text located outside the text, is misleading. This lack of centre becomes the explicit concern of the text as a messenger boy in the office takes out his matchbox and thoughtfully lights his cigar. The text continues: 'I have often thought since on looking back over that strange time that it was that small act, trivial in itself, that striking of that match, that determined the whole aftercourse of both our lives' (177). The monotonous repetition of 'that' confronts us with the impossibility of fixing a moment of presence outside language which would ground the text. This impossibility entails not only that the premises of naturalism and realism are incoherent but also that the division between author and text cannot be sustained. The sentence which comments on the striking of the match contains the word 'that' in three distinct grammatical guises. Four of its occurrences are as a demonstrative, but what they demonstrate, in their repetition, is that it is hopeless to link sign to referent outside a system of difference. Each 'that' invites a further 'that' as the world endlessly subdivides into a meaningless catalogue of demonstratives. This ruination of the referential powers of language, similar to the process at work in the lists of the Cyclops section, is emphasised in the occurrence of 'that' as the restrictive relative specifying 'that striking of that match' as 'that determined the whole aftercourse of both our lives'. The function of a restrictive relative clause is to denote a limitation on the reference of the antecedent. But in this case the limitation, in its all-embracing nature, is no limitation at all. As the demonstratives increase the power of the microscope of language and the relative produces a telescopic view, the event escapes our control. The sentence provides a perfect example of a controlling meta-language which promises a position to a subject. However, its exaggerated form and its place in the text subvert this promise and delineate the sentence's own structure, the structure of a control that the text is in the process of dissolving.

If naturalism assumed the ability to record events without any selection, this sentence demonstrates that events take their place within a selection already operated by language.

The other occurrence of 'that' is to subordinate the indirect statement to 'I have often thought'. The difficulty, however, is to locate the referent of the 'I'. Is this Stephen as the future author that he is to become looking back on the significance of a particular event? Such a belief would have to rest on the realist assumption that there are significant moments in a life. This position, unfortunately, is undermined by the facts of language that the text is forcing on our attention. If the description of an event can always be further refined then it becomes impossible to isolate a moment in the past to which significance can be attributed. To describe the past is not to map language against reality but to seek reality in the significant repetitions that bear witness to our constitution. Stephen Dedalus and James Joyce cannot be held apart; neither one is the cause of the other. What can be said (in all its circularity) is that James Joyce is articulated in the writing of Stephen Dedalus. In the Aeolus section it becomes impossible to hold apart the characters on the page and the novelist who is writing them and, as if in acknowledgement, it is in this section that the text begins a set of humorous references to Joyce as the author. These references enjoy their own status of temporal confusion: Joyce is the writer who is writing the text so that the text will produce the writer who can write the text and so on. One such allusion can be found in Professor MacHugh's reference to Antisthenes. Although Stephen may recognise that he, too, is as bitter against himself as he is against others, only Joyce knows that he will go on to award the palm of beauty to Penelope. In addition characters from *Dubliners* begin to make their appearance in the text (on page 159 Gabriel Conroy is referred to) and the parable of the plums which Stephen relates at the end of the section could easily take its place as one of the stories of spiritual paralysis.

The text itself, in its activity as writing, offers an alternative to the paralysis of Dublin and, particularly, the paralysis threatened by journalism. Bloom, as he stands behind the foreman and watches the presses turning, thinks: 'Now if he got paralysed there and no one knew how to stop them they'd clank on and on the same, print it over and over and up and back' (151). It is Myles Crawford who makes the link explicit when he tries to tempt Stephen into using his writing talents in the newspaper, with the promise that together they will paralyse Europe (172). The discourse of popular journalism constantly centres itself in the evident reality of ideology and can produce nothing but the nauseous repetition of stereotypes. If, however, there is no centre within the text then the space between reader and text becomes open and a process of reading, involving an investigation of the construction of significance, becomes possible.

It becomes obvious as we read past the opening sections that the stream of consciousness techniques must not be understood as providing some final reality in which we can centre the text but, as Joyce told Gilbert, the bridge across which he could march his troops; the troops in question being so many different discourses. Indeed we can read *Ulysses* from Telemachus to Hades as a demonstration of subjectivity, as a pattern of languages constantly appropriating new discourses and losing others. Just as Aristotle, Swift, Shakespeare and others circulate in Stephen's mind providing the sentences with which he experiences the world and himself, so Bloom's mind is composed of snatches of the planter's handbill, Matcham's masterstroke and popularising scientific works. Joyce made this point when Valery Larbaud, then in the process of translating *Ulysses*, asked him if quotations should go between quotation marks. Joyce replied that 'the fewer quotation marks the better' and that even without them the reader 'will know early in the book that S.D's mind is full like everyone else's of borrowed words' (letter to Valery Larbaud, 4 June 1928).

It is from the Aeolus section, however, that it becomes impossible to specify with any precision to whom words belong unless they are explicitly uttered as speech. In Scylla and Charybdis, for example, we come across Stephen's familiar tones voicing the following thought: 'I believe, O Lord, help my unbelief. That is, help me to believe or help me to unbelieve? Who helps to believe? *Egomen*. Who to unbelieve? Other chap' (275). These enigmatic words are glossed by Gifford and Seidman's *Notes for Joyce*:

> *Egomen* – involves a pun on the magazine, *The Egoist*, which began instalment publication of *A Portrait of the Artist as a Young Man* on 2 February 1914, thus helping Joyce to 'believe' (in himself). This would make the 'Other chap' among others, George Roberts, the Dublin publisher and bookseller, who had been so timid about publishing *Dubliners*. *The Egoist* was founded by Dora Marsden as the *Freewoman* in 1911; the *New Freewoman* in 1913; then, urged by Ezra Pound and other *men* to 'mark the character of your paper as an organ of individualists of both sexes, and of the individualist principle in every department of life', she changed the title to *The Egoist*, i.e. Ego-men.

What this makes clear, as indeed does most criticism of *Ulysses*, is that the text cannot be regarded as a closed and self-sufficient unit of meaning for it constantly refers outside itself in a set of random allusions (in this case to events which take place 10 years after the time of the diegesis). It is this element of randomness which differentiates the text's relation to the author with the one that Stephen himself proposes to hold between Shakespeare and his plays. Stephen will not admit the existence of the random, for like the movement of the signifier, it threatens his position as self-determining centre of his world. But, in one of the major contradictions of the text, it is only the acceptance of chance that will allow him to write, because his fixed position is incompatible with writing itself. At the beginning of the Scylla and Charybdis section, Stephen is constantly trying to fix his 'I' in a stable enounced, but the enunciation keeps multiplying the pronoun as he decides whether or not he should pay back the money he owes Russell:

> How now, sirrah, that pound he lent you when you were hungry?

Marry, I wanted it.

Take thou this noble.

Go to! You spent most of it in Georgina Johnson's bed, clergyman's daughter. Agenbite of inwit.

Do you intend to pay it back?

O, yes.

When? Now?

Well . . . no.

When, then?

I paid my way. I paid my way.

Steady on. He's from beyant Boyne water. The northeast corner. You owe it.

Wait. Five months. Molecules all change. I am other I now. Other I got pound.

Buzz. Buzz.

But I, entelechy, form of forms, am I by memory because under everchanging forms.

I that sinned and prayed and fasted.

A child Conmee saved from pandies.

I, I, and I. I.

A.E.I.O.U. (242–3)

Stephen's longing to establish an immutable 'I' for himself is paralleled by his attempt to allocate Shakespeare a definite position in the plays. Stephen wishes to centre Shakespeare's life in the moment when Anne Hathaway tumbled him in the cornfield and then to centre the plays in turn through the interpretation of *Hamlet*. For Stephen, *Hamlet* must be read from the position of the ghost, from the character which he imagines that Shakespeare acted and from whose situation he constructs the meaning of Shakespeare's life and plays. In this search for meaning, Stephen must ignore chance as depriving a life of the coherence necessary for any interpretation. When John Eglington has the temerity to introduce chance into the discussion, 'The world believes that Shakespeare made a mistake and got out of it as quickly and as best he could', Stephen angrily splutters, 'Bosh! A man of genius makes no mistakes. His errors are volitional and are the portals of discovery.' Stephen wishes to tie every event within a life to the will and thus avoid the admission of chance. The next line of the text, however, emphasises the arbitrary when it mockingly declares 'Portals of discovery opened to let in the quaker librarian, soft-creakfooted, bald, eared and assiduous'. As Stephen sits in the corner of the library at the imaginary centre of his world, that world is constantly being altered by events outside his control. It is chance that will confront him with Bloom later in the day as it is chance that brings Bloom through the library doors a few minutes later.

The neurotic's denial of chance is at one with the denial of the signifier. Both threaten identity, leaving it at the mercy of others' actions and others' voices. Stephen's impossible determination to be the centre of his world finds linguistic unease in the debate between English and Gaelic which weaves in and out of the discussion in the library. The offer of a choice of signifiers contaminates the certainty of the signified. It is this contamination which ruins Stephen's voice as a medium in which the signifiers efface themselves. He complains that 'I am tired of my voice, the voice of Esau. My kingdom for a drink' (271). The voice of Esau, as the Bible tells us, is the voice that cannot establish identity, that is not sufficient to ensure paternal recognition. Stephen's difficulty is that he cannot find a figure that can occupy the place of the father. If the real father's weakness prevents an identification, the imaginary father of the nation is an equally impotent being who lacks both a living language and political independence. Neither can function as an origin secure enough to guarantee his present identity, abandoning him to the mercy of chance and language.

It is this reality of chance and language that Stephen's theory of Shakespeare, a theory of origin and identity, repudiates. Stephen's rejection of his own theory signals a liberation from the neurotic problematic within which he had constructed Shakespeare's biography. Caught in the contradiction that his theory must hold for all of Shakespeare's plays, but that he has not read all the plays, Stephen laughs 'to free his mind from his mind's bondage' (272). It is with this laugh that he disowns the attempt to characterise Shakespeare's work as a representation of Shakespeare's life. Shakespeare is no longer the controlling subject measuring word against world but becomes the fugitive subject articulated from character to character; his identity is the movement of difference that constitutes the plays:

> He is all in all.
> – He is, Stephen said. The boy of act one is the mature man of act five. All in all. In *Cymbeline*, in *Othello* he is bawd and cuckold. He acts and is acted on. Lover of an ideal or a per-version, like José he kills the real Carmen. His unremitting intellect is the hornmad Iago ceaselessly willing that the moor in him shall suffer (272–3).

Freud's distinction between *Witz* and *Humor* can provide an understanding of the liberation that Stephen's laugh produces. The laugh of *Humor* is produced by the superego at the expense of the ego. Mulligan's jokes are examples of *Humor*, conferring power and laughter through their implied certainty as to what is really the case. It is hardly surprising that his witticisms are so uniformly sexual, the certainty implied revolving around the possession of the phallus and knowledge. Stephen's laugh, however, is not produced by a simple mistake but in the realisa-tion that any statement is always mistaken in so far as there is always more information available. This recognition of the im-possibility of total knowledge entails an awareness of the limits of language. Any description of the world is always the product of choice and limitation but those choices and limits are denied in the form of the description. The laugh of *Witz* is produced with the demonstration of the ridiculous claims of language to place us in a position of knowledge. *Witz* produces a moment of liberation from our necessary egocentricity. The practices of *Ulysses* accomplish this liberation as the reader is unable to find a position of knowledge in the text.

It is the ignoring of language in communication that allows the production of a position of knowledge. But such ignorance is impossible for Stephen. The demand of the mother that he take his place in an Irish and Catholic world is constantly exceeded by the desire that binds him to her. Mulligan, with his rhymes and phallic imagery, stands as one example of the world of communication, the singers in the Ormond Bar are another. They (in the world of voices) are opposed by Bloom the writer, an opposition which is given explicit sexual point by the references to membranes which run through the Sirens section. Bloom, as he sits writing in the dining room, is contrasted with Ben Dollard who is singing. But whereas the singer will enter the body of another with his voice (in an analogue of Boylan's entry into Molly), the writer receives his pleasure in an infinite game of hide and seek with himself, each stage of the game producing new participants. Those who wish to burst the membrane and affirm their own presence, Dollard and Boylan, are contrasted with Bloom and the reader playing on the surface of the text with their own absence. The violent and narcissistic nature of the voice is spelt out on page 348:

> – Sure you'd burst the tympanum of her ear, man, Mr Dedalus said through smoke aroma, with an organ like yours.
> In bearded abundant laughter Dollard shook upon the keyboard. He would.
> – Not to mention another membrane, Father Cowley added.

The identification of tympanum and hymen is made explicit in this passage. Later on in the section Bloom compares the vellum paper on which he is writing (vellum once meant the parchment made from skin)[1] with the hymen in very different

[1] The word vellum seems also to give a reference to velum. This word, in English, refers to the membrane on the soft palate which is articulated in the production of guttural sounds. More tendentiously, through its etymology (Latin 'velum' – a sail) the word links up with the constant references to 'sails' and 'veils' in the text. The French word 'voile' which translates both meanings is of crucial importance for Mallarmé. Indeed the cluster of wave, sea, siren, veil imagery suggests that the whole of The Sirens could be read as a

terms:

'Blank face. Virgin should say: or fingered only. Write something on it: page' (368). Bloom's desire to write on the membrane rather than burst through it is an evasion of the pathological masculinity that cripples the drinkers in the bar. His evasions are the result of the difficulty, which he shares with Stephen (but with which he has achieved a compromise) of filling the place of the father. Virag's suicide, and the change of family name, are clear admissions of the real father's radical insufficiency and Bloom's confused religions and nationalities make both throne and altar equally inadequate substitutes. Bloom cannot secure an identification which would ward off lack and is thus submitted to/can enjoy the articulation of his desire across the movement of signifiers, along elaborate fantasies. This submission to the signifier is a submission to writing and writing functions, throughout Joyce's work, as the very exemplar of perversion. The crucial feature of perversion, as Circe demonstrates, is the instability of sexual position. As writing commences and sends back novel messages to hitherto unnoticed receivers, the unitary subject dissolves into a play of many voices. In the reciprocity which founds desire – my desire is the desire for the other but it is also the other's desire (the place I am allocated by the other) – gender alternates with voice. Active and passive, male and female, every speaker is articulated as both subject and object. It is this fact that the pervert acknowledges in fantasy but it is the moment at which the fantasy is arrested, fixed, that the pervert can save his identity, his phallus, and enter the realm of communication and knowledge. This, of course, is what Bloom does. After masturbating on the beach he joins the drinkers in the house of Horne (the phallic connotations of that name have been emphasised by Lenehan's question to Boylan, 'Got the horn or what?' (344).

So far the concept of perversion has been used in simple opposition to neurosis. The pervert is articulated around the lack that the neurotic refuses to acknowledge. It is clear, how-

prolonged meditation on Mallarmé's comparison of writing and the sexual act.

ever, that Joyce's writing demands further distinctions within the concept of perversion. That is to say we must distinguish between a perverse structure which, while suspending the either/or of sexual difference and investigating the non-disjunctive nature of discourse, undertakes this suspension and investigation only with the guarantee that the process will be ended and denied, and, on the other hand, a perversion so radical that there is never any question of arresting the process. The first is the fetishistic structure that we saw at work in Balzac's text and although the young Joyce holds the disjunction open for longer and longer, a close will always loom as a possibility unless the disjunction is endlessly multiplied. It is with the reworking of the text in Circe, a reworking which refuses any possibility of an end to the book, that bisexuality undermines any simple phallic position. It is only with the production of the female voice within the male that the phallic position is finally abandoned. If we pass from the neurosis of Stephen to the perversion of Bloom, it is not until we reach the radical refusal of position in Penelope that we leave behind the world of representation.

But if Bloom finally arrests the process of the signifier, he also provides the initial movement of the text. If the voice of the singers in the Ormond Bar affirms a presence and an identity that Stephen longs for, Bloom is the ear that deconstructs the presence into difference. As ear Bloom finds himself opposed to the eye, which provides a privileged site for the imaginary, and which is opposed to the ear throughout *Finnegans Wake* as well as *Ulysses*. The eye is the organ with which the singers confront the world as they forget the ear in the illusion of pure presence. Similarly in Cyclops, the aggressive world of drink and communication from which Bloom is excluded is embodied by the one-eyed citizen (it can be noticed that the Citizen's deformity turns him into a huge phallic pun). In the Ormond Bar, the barmaids simply act as mirrors to the masculine world. The various equations of the Sirens between eye, voice, phallus, nationalism and religion find particular emphasis in their reflection by Lydia Douce as she listens to the song of the Croppy Boy:

On the smooth jutting beerpull laid Lydia hand lightly, plumply, leave it to my hands. All lost in pity for croppy. Fro, to: to, fro: over the polished knob (she knows his eyes, my eyes, her eyes) her thumb and finger passed in pity: passed, repassed and, gently touching, then slid so smoothly, slowly down, a cool firm white enamel baton protruding through their sliding ring (369).

In order to confirm male power, women can only function as mirrors; they must deny their own sexuality. If Bloom manages to ignore the mirrors of the Sirens he finally succumbs to an arresting of the signifiers in Nausicaa. Gerty McDowell's existence is an attempt to turn herself into the fetish prescribed by the women's magazine discourse that articulates her experience (it is the same discourse used by Miss Douce and Miss Kennedy).[1] It is on the beach that Bloom, if only through a prolonged detour, reaffirms the power of the phallus. That this power is dependent on a repression of female sexuality, and above all of female genitality, is made obvious through a variety of devices. Firstly there is Gerty's repeated attempts to ignore the onset of her period, an effort which reduplicates her struggle to remain in control of the flow of language. In Nausicaa we can read the preservation of the subject-predicate form and the denial of the body as elements of the same structure. Secondly, one can notice the constant references to the Virgin which punctuate Gerty's monologue. Stephen has already analysed the conscious begetting of the son by the father as the crucial feature of religion. What the text emphasises is that such a conscious begetting involves a disavowal of the mother's sexuality. The virgin as mother bears witness to the power of the phallic wor(l)d of communication: the voice of the father shatters the tympanum to produce the son.[2] This direct conception avoids

[1] Fritz Senn makes the same point in a fascinating essay on Nausicaa (Senn 1974). Senn points out that it is not only the barmaids who share Gerty's language but also Molly. Molly's speech differs from Gerty's, however, in her abandonment of the carefully ordered form that Gerty is so anxious to retain.

[2] When Ben Dollard reappears in Circe it is in response to the cry by Virag 'He burst her tympanum' (637). This phrase, which appears amongst a cluster of allusions to Christian medieval legends, is a reference to the medieval

any risk of a contamination by lack that contact with the female sexual organs might produce. Finally, Gerty's limp marks her as less than perfect, an example of the inferior version of the male that women must represent in a phallocentric order. Before this female denial of female sexuality Bloom becomes the powerful phallic 'I', eyes, and masturbates.

By the end of the Nausicaa section both Stephen and Bloom have been exhausted by the voyage of the text. If both find access to the fetishistic world of communication difficult because of the impossibility of locating an identity in familial, national, or religious terms, both are finally trapped within a male narcissism which prevents them ever fully articulating a desire which would confound any notion of identity. It is true that they both retain the characteristics that have been assigned to them by the text and with which they dissociate themselves from others but this dissociation is now at the level of action and emotion. The activity of writing has been completely taken over by the text and it is only the writer/reader who is still voyaging through sense. The reader, having voyaged through language, has been displaced from the world of communication in which the medical students revel. The Oxen of the Sun takes us through the history of the English language but a language which has now become pure system. With each change of discourse, the figures before us reform like elements in a kaleidoscope, except that, unlike the viewer of a kaleidoscope, our position too is alterable: subject and object are both mere effects of this anatomy of discourse. Language has been set free from the fixity of position into that pure flow that was prefigured earlier in the mathematical symbols that moved across the page 'in grave morrice' (33).

This liberation of language is more radical than that in Joyce's earlier texts where a fetishistic disavowal allowed both a submission to an experience of language and the security of a

---

belief that at the Conception the Word of God penetrated the Virgin Mary's ear. Mulligan thinks that his emphasis on a phallic sexuality is irreligious but *Ulysses* makes clear that it is the degraded successor of a logic of repression.

dominant position. If *Dubliners* and *A Portrait* functioned in terms of an ever more radical 'suspense' of the disjunctive nature of discourse, there was still the possibility of re-establishing criteria of truth and falsity. In the finale of The Oxen of the Sun, the welter of slang and sound grants no privilege to contemporary English as against past or future, there is no longer any extra-discursive criterion of truth. It is the dominance of repetition in *Ulysses* which accomplishes this change in the reader's position. The recurrence of certain key phrases testify constantly to the indestructible materiality of the signifier and to its dominance over the signified (each time a phrase recurs its meaning changes with the environment). The trace, the wake, of the letter is never finally eradicated, a thought that occurs to Bloom as he prepares to blot his letter to Martha Clifford and reflects that his letter might be read off the blotting pad (361). Bloom's immediate reaction is to think that this could form the basis for a prize detective story, a reaction dependent on the written trace left by his earlier reading of Matcham's masterstroke. In a flood of repetitions the text immediately recalls Mrs Purefoy and U.P: up and, as Bloom reflects that language is littered with quotations from Shakespeare, the text rewrites two lines from the library sequence on page 259. Just as Bloom is composed of the written traces he has appropriated, we, too, are composed in and by the text. To read any novel is to trade flesh against word, the repetitions of *Ulysses* make certain that we cannot ignore that transaction.

The repetitions mark the text of *Ulysses* as written and allow different meanings to attach to the signifiers. It is exactly this possibility of new meanings that is the possibility of desire speaking. The word escapes the control of the speaking subject in so far as it is always open to new definitions and it is in these new definitions that desire finds expression. Desire is the passage along the metonymy of signifiers and it is in those moments when the signifier is no longer under the domination of the signified that desire speaks: that 'it' talks there where 'I' have lost control. Thus the nonsense of a verbal parapraxis is the slip in the metonymic chain which points to the waking of desire. If the movement from signifier to signifier is the movement of fantasy, this movement always comes back to consciousness as fixed, as enounced, a certain meaning, a definite signified. The signifier, however, involves the subject in relations of which he knows nothing. As the body moves along the signifying chain, it takes up all the positions offered to it. To use language is to risk identity, gender and position as we always say more than we mean. Freud's analysis of the common fantasy which finds expression as 'A child is being beaten' demonstrates the wealth of desire articulated in a single phrase. The sentence allows the unconscious adoption of the position of beater and beaten as well as the explicit role of observer. The changes of voice and person necessary for such identification are contained in the verbal paradigm which gives meaning to the original phrase.

In Circe, the whole text of *Ulysses* is taken up and repeated, a repetition which allows the speaking of desire. Circe is the text's unconscious as the events of the day get reworked in Nightown.[1] But it is not simply the text that is re-articulated in Circe but also the reader as words, already appropriated, return bearing different meanings and values. It has been argued that the movement of writing, of perversion, constitutes an insistent pressure of the feminine that threatens a male narcissism desperate to purge itself of the taint of difference. Such masculine narcissism is endangered when the prostitute Zoe takes the fetish from Bloom, the fetish that he has earlier claimed from his mother's skirts. The loss of the fetish, an analogue of the reader's loss of position, allows writing to be experienced at its most corrosive as Bloom becomes a woman. The confusion of the notion of sexual identity throws in question yet another of the basic oppositions which maintain truth and falsity as a disjunction. The bisexuality in question does not involve some perfect imaginary union of a disjunct (which would spell the imaginary end of language as difference disap-

[1] The transformations at work in Circe recall those processes which Freud describes as basic to the working of the unconscious: condensation and displacement. Hugh Kenner comes close to a correct description when in an essay on Circe he characterises it as 'a nearly accidental psychoanalysis, wholly lacking an analyst' (Kenner 1974, p. 360).

peared in an ideal Platonic moment). Rather, as in Freud's
theory of bisexuality, it implies an infinite and vertiginous regression as Bloom and Bella reflect each other in an endless hall
of mirrors. As the text succeeds in giving a voice to the woman
in Bloom, it abandons disjunction in favour of a bisexuality
which multiplies identity geometrically.

It is the voicing of female desire, if only in its masculine position, that produces the space for an escape from neurosis. If the
mother's demands to take the place of the father weigh heavier
and heavier on the son, it is their insistence which demonstrates
that place as untenable. Stephen is living the contradiction of
the neurotic: the demand of the mother, which should bury her
desire, bears witness to it. He begs his mother to tell him the
word that is 'known to all men' (682) and that demand is for a
word that will come complete with its own meaning, elimin-
ating the hazardous world of the signifier where he is at the
mercy of chance. But the name he must come to learn is a signifier in excess of a signified, a name in excess of its bearer: the
Name of the Father. Stephen must come to kill the priest and
king in his head because the mother testifies to their impotence.
He must learn their names lest the corpses continue to rot on
their hollow thrones.

It is with the experience of the writing of Circe that the
mother's desire can be disinterred, a raising of the dead which
allows the possibility of life. To articulate that desire, in its
insistence and excentricity, is to come to know death, the an-
nihilation of the conscious subject in the system of language,
the loss of identity in those reciprocities of desire that find us
always in another's place. The moment of darkness which Stephen passes through as he breaks the lamp is a liberation from
time and demand. This liberation is rhymed in grotesque and
inverse form with the hanging of the Croppy Boy which takes
place a few pages after Stephen's exit from the brothel (691).
The Croppy Boy moves through the pages of *Ulysses* as a warning to Stephen of the fate that awaits him if he assumes the identity that the mother urges on him. The story of the song is
simple: a poor peasant, off to fight for Ireland, wishes to confess

his sins. Most grievous of these is a single failure to remember to pray for his mother on passing her grave. As he finishes his confession, he is startled to find that the priest he had imagined to be listening is in fact a British soldier. The soldier orders that he be hanged without delay.

The Croppy Boy's mistake reveals the true identity of priest and king but the simple patriot is unable to grasp this. Furthermore the Croppy Boy actually confesses to that which he should relish as freedom: forgetting to pray for his mother's rest. The Croppy Boy stands for all the disastrous demands made in Ireland and from which the only release is death. A death which must take place in reality because demand represses the possibility of any symbolic extinction. It is such a symbolic death that marks the child's entry to the order of language as it hears its name articulated in a situation from which it is excluded: when the parents speak to each other. The mother's refusal to exclude the child bars the world of the signifier and desire; death becomes impossible before a perpetual demand. The Croppy Boy achieves death and, in that moment, the signifier returns against the mother's demand: 'Horhot ho hray ho rhother's hest' (forgot to pray for his mother's rest). But this return is as mechanical as the orgasm which sends gouts of sperm flowing over the cobblestones. It is a purely physical reaction of a body severed from consciousness rather than the extinction of consciousness in a body of language. It is a death of the second sort that Circe literally spells out and the antithesis between the two deaths is emphasised by Stephen's cry of 'Nothung!' (not hung like the Croppy) at the climax of the chapter. It is small wonder that Joyce suffered so much strain while writing Circe and that he placed this episode under the protection of Hermes in his letters to Budgen. The God of communication ensures a way back to the world of demand and also to a masculine position. Joyce notes that Circe 'is the only occasion on which Ulysses is not helped by Minerva but by her male counterpart or inferior' (letter to Frank Budgen, Michaelmas 1920).

The end of the text – the Nostos – can be considered as a

persistent refusal to close the text, a refusal which in the same way, but on a grand scale, duplicates that refusal of closure which I have indicated throughout Joyce's work. In the Eumaeus episode the reader might expect to be given the significance of the day's events and Bloom, manfully, attempts to do that by writing the short story he has been contemplating all day and which he entitles '*My Experiences*, let us say, *in a Cabman's Shelter* (750). Despite, however, the hopeful conglomeration of characters at Skin-the-Goat's, nothing emerges until the last paragraph when, as Stephen and Bloom walk off and begin a discussion of the book's themes, 'sirens, enemies of man's reason, mingled with a number of other topics of the same category, usurpers' (775–6), we, the readers, are firmly placed outside the *tête-à-tête*. Similarly Ithaca, in its surplus of answers, provides no place for the reader from which the text will make sense.

Ithaca, as Joyce said, is the end (if not the close) of the book (Letter to Harriet Shaw Weaver, 7 October 1921), for Penelope is simply the movement of the book all over again, the movement to writing and the speaking of female desire through a male pen. With the breakdown of the subject-predicate form, the text becomes an enunciation which will not settle into the form of an enounced. The clichés which make up the content of Molly's thought are unimportant as we achieve the motion of the signifier towards which we have been voyaging. All that perhaps should be noted is the savagery of this text, a savagery directed against that fetishism of the penis that Freud remarked as typical in our society. It is often said that there is no slaughter of the suitors in Joyce's version of Ulysses despite Joyce's explicit comment to Budgen that he intended to place such a slaughter in Penelope: 'At first I had not thought of the slaughter of the suitors as in Ulysses' character. Now I see it can be there too. I am going to leave the last word with Molly Bloom' (letter to Frank Budgen, 10 December 1920).

Homer's *Odyssey* finishes with the affirmation of Odysseus' phallic power as he bends the bow that has defied the suitors. This action, which returns Penelope to her rightful place and brings the story to an end, could find no place with the strategy of *Ulysses*. But to have Penelope herself as the destroyer of the phallic pretensions of the suitors continues the process of the work. No Gerty McDowell, Molly refuses to conform to the wishes of men and as such she is fatal to a fetishism predicated on a denial of female desire. Much speculation has been devoted to what happens after the end of *Ulysses*, but no one seems to have remarked that what is certain is Boylan's death. Not that Blazes will physically expire, but, like the other suitors that Molly names, his being is mortally wounded by a voice that will not be reduced to sense and a body that will not be reduced to a lack.

# 6

# A Political Reading of *Finnegans Wake*

It has been argued that Joyce's texts grant a primacy to the material of language over the fugitive meanings that attach to it. As such they offer a different experience and have different political consequences, from the classic realist text which they displace. The realist text is organised to confer an identity on the reader through an exclusion of language. We become deaf to the shifting of the signifier as we become fixated in meaning. As we read Joyce, however, a surplus of meaning enables us to hear the crowd of voices that compose us. Voices that bear witness to the incompatible discourses that have traversed our flesh. Joyce's formal experiments deal with our very substance and when Beckett states that Joyce's writing 'is not about something, it is that something itself' (Beckett 1929, p. 14), he points not to an empty formalism but to an encounter with those constitutive processes that render us sexed and civil subjects. Joyce's writing concentrates on the relations of language, desire and power; of discourse, sexuality and politics.

It is these relations that produce the incessant repetitions of *Finnegans Wake*, the inevitable return to a network of significations which are different but the same, mobile but static. *Finnegans Wake* turns around the connections between writing and sexuality, around the mother's letter which will reveal the secrets of the father's desire. But these connections are inseparable from politics, as is indicated by the continual confusion of the mother's letter with a variety of famous letters from the history of Irish nationalism. The whole tradition of Joycean criticism has involved a quasi-deliberate inattention to these political aspects of Joyce's texts. The reality of Irish politics is ignored in favour of considering Parnell's place in Joyce's personal mythology, a reduction of politics to the personal which is evident in a book like Hélène Cixous's *The Exile of James Joyce*. Cixous was the first critic to give any prominence to the political content of Joyce's Italian letters to Stanislaus, but she manages to place this content within a psychological account of Joyce's construction of roles. Philip F. Herring's paper on Joyce's politics at the second Joyce symposium is an example of the prevailing assumptions on this topic: 'Institutions were important only because his personal reaction against them helped to define his artistic consciousness' (Herring 1972, pp. 4–5). The most serious consequence of this psychologisation of Joyce's politics is the undervaluing of Joyce's commitment to socialism before the First World War and Herring can once again be taken as typical when he writes that 'Joyce contented himself with opposing the forces that made his exile necessary; that those same forces (British imperialism, a Church hierarchy preoccupied with its own power, provincial narrowness of mind) had been condemned by his fellow Irish socialists as largely responsible for the poverty, emigration and spiritual stagnation of the Irish people during past centuries was for him merely coincidental' (ibid, p. 10).

This attitude to Joyce's politics is often the result of an ignorance of Irish and European politics in the first two decades of this century. Joyce's refusal to visit the Irish Free State, or even to surrender his British passport in exchange for an Irish one, is not the evident sign of a lack of interest in Irish affairs that it has seemed to so many critics. For many Irishmen, not least the members of the I.R.A., who have refused to recognise its existence for nearly sixty years, the establishment of the Free State was the most grievous political defeat. Similarly Joyce's abandonment of politics after the outbreak of the First World War must be understood in terms of the political options then available. The poem 'Dooleysprudence' which Joyce wrote in

Zurich in 1916, can be read in the context of the failure of the
Socialist parties to prevent, or even oppose, the war, although
most critics have preferred to read it as a product of Joyce's 'individualism'.

> Who is the man when all the gallant nations run to war
> Goes home to have his dinner by the very first cable car
> And as he eats his cantelope contorts himself in mirth
> To read the blatant bulletins of the rulers of the earth?
>> It's Mr Dooley,
>> Mr Dooley,
>> The coolest chap our country ever knew
>> 'They are out to collar
>> The dime and dollar'
>> Says Mr Dooley-ooley-ooley-oo.

> Who is the funny fellow who declines to go to church
> Since pope and priest and parson left the poor man in the
> lurch
> And taught their flocks the only way to save all human souls
> Was piercing human bodies through with dumdum bullet-
> holes?
>> It's Mr Dooley,
>> Mr Dooley,
>> The mildest man our country ever knew
>> 'Who will release us
>> From Jingo Jesus'
>> Prays Mr Dooley-ooley-ooley-oo.

> Who is the meek philosopher who doesn't care a damn
> About the yellow peril or problem of Siam
> And disbelieves that British Tar is water from life's fount
> And will not gulp the gospel of the German on the Mount?
>> It's Mr Dooley,
>> Mr Dooley,
>> The broadest brain our country ever knew
>> 'The curse of Moses

On both your houses'
Cries Mr Dooley-ooley-ooley-oo.

Who is the cheerful imbecile who lights his long chibouk
With pages of the pandect, penal code and Doomsday Book
And wonders why bald justices are bound by law to wear
A toga and a wig made out of someone else's hair?
  It's Mr Dooley,
  Mr Dooley,
  The finest fool our country ever knew
  'They took that toilette
  From Pontius Pilate'
  Thinks Mr Dooley-ooley-ooley-oo.

Who is the man who says he'll go the whole and perfect hog
Before he pays the income tax or license for a dog
And when he licks a postage stamp regards with smiling
scorn
  The face of king or emperor or snout of unicorn?
  It's Mr Dooley,
  Mr Dooley,
  The wildest wag our country ever knew
  'O my poor tummy
  His backside gummy!'
  Moans Mr Dooley-ooley-ooley-oo.

Who is the tranquil gentleman who won't salute the State
Or serve Nebuchadnezzar or proletariat
But thinks that every son of man has quite enough to do
To paddle down the stream of life his personal canoe?
  It's Mr Dooley,
  Mr Dooley,
  The wisest wight our country ever knew
  'Poor Europe ambles
  Like sheep to shambles'
  Sighs Mr Dooley-ooley-ooley-oo.

This poem indicates a refusal of politics but one that, in the last verse, is explicitly tied to the war. As Europe ambles like sheep to shambles, and as Ireland prepares for six years of civil strife, Joyce writes *Ulysses*. The critical tradition has identified Joyce with Dooley and seen Joyce's immature attachment to socialism give way to a mature individualism. But this perspective ignores the time and place of Joyce's writing. It ignores the fact that Dooley is consciously a political subversive.

Along with a lack of interest in Joyce's politics, there has been a general failure by linguists or literary critics to deal seriously with Joyce's use of language. Since Margaret Schlauch's fascinating article in the magazine *Science and Society* in 1939, there have been very few articles on this topic produced within the considerable academic framework of Joyce studies.[1] Politics and language are what lie buried beneath the endless studies on the symbolic correspondences, on the autobiography, on myth, on the meaning of the works. It is to questions of the relations between politics and language in *Finnegans Wake* that I wish to

---

[1] It is the introduction of the reader into the systematic order of discourse in *Finnegans Wake*, which has made the book so intractable to linguists. Recently Strother Purdy has made an admirable effort to come to terms with the *Wake*'s language in '*Mind your genderous: Toward a* Wake *Grammar*' (Purdy 1972). Purdy's interesting researches are, however, doomed to partial failure in so far as he is committed to a philosophy of language as communication and to using a theory of language which ignores the subject's positioning in discourse. Any account of *Finnegans Wake* must explain the effect that F. G. Asenjo tried to specify in an idealist vocabulary in his article 'The General Problem of Sentence Structure: An Analysis prompted by the loss of subject in *Finnegans Wake*' (Asenjo 1964). Asenjo tried to explain how each word within the sentence could take up the role of subject with regard to the rest of the sentence but his account is held back by an ideology of expressivity that runs through his account. Margaret Schlauch's article 'The Language of James Joyce' made the point that personal connections of the reader were permitted by the language structure: 'Joyce demands more active participation from his public than any other writer I can recall' (Schlauch 1939, p. 490). Lacking a linguistics of discourse it is not yet possible to give a theoretical account of how language works in *Finnegans Wake*. What is certain is that it will never be a question of *applying* linguistic theories to the *Wake*. Rather it is a question of using Joyce's experiments to elaborate methods for the analysis of discourse. It is not impossible to envisage a time when *Finnegans Wake* will be an essential part of any linguistics course. Any future advances in this area will lean heavily on the insights, if not the vocabulary, of Anthony Burgess's *Joysprick*, a work produced outside any academic framework.

devote this chapter but before turning to these substantial questions I want to indicate the importance of a consideration of Joyce's politics at the most *evident* level.

Emblematically one could recall the critical reception afforded to the metaphor which Joyce used to illuminate his progress around Europe. Hundreds of thousands of words have been devoted to glossing this *exile*. It has been construed as the artist holding himself away from his people, as the sensitive soul escaping the provincial deadness of Ireland, as the heretic fleeing the Catholic Church. But what is never investigated is the real basis of this imaginary figure: the economic subservience in which Ireland was held by the imperial power of England. This subservience has ensured that since the famine, exile has been the normal condition of the Irish man and woman:

> . . . although there were some parts of Ireland – most notoriously, Mayo – where there was enough inferior land available for the population actually to increase after the famine, in the more fertile areas often the only alternative to pauperism for the landless man was emigration. Emigration, therefore, there had to be, emigration which in one form or another was to form part of the very fabric of Irish society during the succeeding hundred years (Lyons 1973, p. 45).

The difficulty of getting a job in Ireland was one of the crucial factors in Joyce's decision to leave Ireland and that he was aware of how he shared this fate with his countrymen and women is made clear by the words he addressed to his fellow Triestinos on this subject:

> Finally, in the field of practical affairs this pejorative conception of Ireland is given the lie by the fact that when the Irishman is found outside Ireland in another environment, he very often becomes a respected man. The economic and intellectual conditions that prevail in his own country do not permit the development of individuality. The soul of the country is weakened by centuries of useless struggles and

broken treaties, and individual initiative is paralysed by the influence and admonitions of the church, while its body is manacled by the police, the tax office, and the garrison. No one who has any self-respect stays in Ireland, but flees afar as though from a country that has undergone the visitation of an angered Jove.

From the time of the Treaty of Limerick, or rather, from the time that it was broken by the English in bad faith, millions of Irishmen have left their native land. These fugitives, as they were centuries ago, are called the wild geese . . . even today, the flight of the wild geese continues. Every year, Ireland, decimated as she already is, loses 60,000 of her sons. From 1850 to the present day, more than 5,000,000 emigrants have left for America, and every post brings to Ireland their inviting letters to friends and relatives at home. The old men, the corrupt, the children, and the poor stay at home, where the double yoke wears another groove in the tamed neck; and around the death bed, where the poor anaemic, almost lifeless body lies in agony, the rulers give orders and the priests administer last rites (CW 171–2).

It is only through a consideration of the economic basis of Joyce's exile that we can understand the uncertainty and irony which is generated around Stephen Dedalus's appeal to exile as the solitary way. An added autobiographical joke has Stephen confiding this to Cranly. For Joyce's friend Byrne, on whom Cranly is based, was also to choose exile when he emigrated to America, six years after Joyce had left Ireland.

It is not only the understanding of such a major theme in Joyce's work that suffers because of the general lack of interest in Joyce's politics. The constant references to politics in Joyce's texts have generally received less attention than those to religion or literature. But these references can add to a given text's connotations in a variety of ways. In the Aeolus section of *Ulysses*, for example, we are treated to the spectacle of the political paralysis of Ireland as the old Parnellites bemoan the speech of the night before. The decline of the papers founded to help the nationalist cause and the windbags that have replaced Parnell are two symptoms of the spread of the disease. But the chapter is interesting in that it moves briefly outside the normal petit-bourgeois world of *Ulysses* and, in that move, it demonstrates a surprisingly clear awareness of the nature and extent of the conservatism that afflicts Ireland. Nannetti, the foreman with whom Bloom discusses the question of the Keyes' advertisement, is one of the few members of the unionised working class who figures in *Ulysses*. He was an M.P. for the nationalist party and was constantly cited as the example of how the nationalist cause embraced all classes. Indeed Nannetti was appointed as liaison officer between the Irish T.U.C. and the nationalist party, and his was a powerful voice within the trade-union movement against the setting up of a separate working-class party. In addition it may not be farfetched to see an anachronistic political allusion in the prominent place assigned to the newspaper boys and the trams of Dublin. In 1913, in an attempt to break the growing power of the Irish Transport and General Workers' Union, which Larkin and Connolly had been so successful in establishing in the previous five years, the Dublin employers organised a lock-out. The Dublin Lock-Out (which provided the bitterest and longest industrial struggle of Irish history and which was the occasion for the foundation of the Irish Citizen Army) turned around the unionisation of the trams and the newspaper delivery boys. The employers were led by William Martin Murphy, a former nationalist M.P.

What I want to suggest by indicating these facts is that the political analysis implicit in the Aeolus section is far more complex than a simple statement that Parnell is dead and gone. The resonances and allusions of this chapter indicate that the paralysis of Irish politics is a result of the illusions about class antagonisms that were fostered by the nationalist ideology. That this was the political analysis arrived at by the young Joyce and that the later literary works imply a similar position is what I wish to argue in these closing chapters. Both the early political analysis and the later literary works were produced within a certain political conjuncture and they can both be understood in political terms. Such an understanding, however, implies a serious concern with both Irish and Italian politics of the time and it is this concern which is lacking in almost all the standard work on Joyce. Ellmann's biography, magnificent achievement that it is, is sadly wanting in its descriptions of Joyce's political beliefs. Joyce's comments are constantly reduced to the ramblings of a great artist: 'Trieste resembled Dublin, too, in its Irredentist movement; the similarity here was so striking that Joyce found he could interest his Italian friends in Irish political parallels, *though no doubt he would have compelled them to listen in any case*' (Ellmann 1959 p. 203; my emphasis). The trivialisation of this last phrase distracts attention from the real political similarities between Ireland and Italy at the turn of the century, similarities so striking that James Connolly learned Italian in America because 'he thought their problems resembled those of the Irish' (Greaves 1972, p. 185).

If, in later works, Ellmann has taken Joyce's political position more seriously, his general disinterest in politics remains constant. In the article on Joyce's politics in *The Consciousness of Joyce*, Ellmann argues that the use of the slogan 'Sinn Fein' in *Ulysses* indicates that Joyce was a supporter of Arthur Griffith in 1922. Joyce's anachronistic use of the slogan (it was formulated about a year after 16 June 1904) and his fictional claim that Bloom had suggested it to Arthur Griffith confer, in a book which is otherwise remarkable for its meticulous accuracy, great significance on the phrase. But to argue that it demonstrates particular support for Griffith is to ignore the particular history of these two words. Griffith's movement, which had known some success in the years 1905–8 (and which Joyce, at the time, had critically supported as the alternative to the traditional nationalist party), was a spent force two or three years after that. The slogan came back to prominence when it became identified with the Easter Rising. But the major components of the Rising, insurrectionary nationalism and revolutionary socialism, had nothing to do with Griffith's movement, nor its policies of abstentionism and protectionism.

After 1916 (during the period that Joyce was writing *Ulysses*), 'Sinn Fein' was not to be identified with Griffith but rather with the political heirs of the Easter Rising, heirs who declared war on the state that Griffith, in 1921, had helped to negotiate into being.

The purpose of these remarks is not to create another context for Joyce in which the texts will finally body forth their true meaning (at long last the political one that those with left-wing sympathies have waited for all along). Rather these considerations are simply designed to disrupt expectations of the non-political nature of Joyce's writing and to allow some new considerations of *Finnegans Wake*. The *Wake* insists constantly on the relations between language and sexuality; on the secrets about the father's encounters in Phoenix Park that the letter will reveal. What has not been sufficiently understood is the political consequences of these considerations of sexuality.

If Stephen in *A Portrait* still considers himself a 'fosterchild' who may find a father worthy to bear the name of Dedalus, the split between bearer and name is made absolute in *Finnegans Wake* as the father becomes the simple permutation of a set of letters. It is the divorce between bearer and name which allows language to signify, but this divorce is necessarily unconscious in any normal use of language. *Finnegans Wake* disrupts any such normal use in order to insist on the divorce. In the imaginary world of the child there is a simple correspondence between sign and referent; the two are magically linked together in a one to one relation. But the word gains its meaning through the differential relations into which it enters on the phonological and semantic levels and not through any relation to its referent. It is the recognition of the systematic nature of language (that names are defined through a set of substitutions; that they find their definition in a nexus of differences rather than a plenitude of being) which is the condition of the use of language. What Joyce offers us in his writing is an experience of what Freud was teaching contemporaneously: that the determining moment in this process is the recognition that the father is no more than a name but that this recognition is buried in an effort to control a possible riot of words.

One can restate this paradox in slightly different terms. As I write, each word finds its sense and meaning through the differential oppositions that define it within the English language. I retain, however, the impression that I am conferring the meanings on the words in the act of writing. This division is the constitutive feature of language and subjectivity and it is a condition of the division that Freud categorised in terms of the conscious and the unconscious, the ego and the id, the 'I' and the 'it'. In the 'I' of the enounced I can locate a secure position but in the enunciation the passage along the material of language offers an endless set of substitutions rather than a fixed position. Thus the importance of the lapsus for Freud because it is at that moment when the subject loses control of his or her discourses that something else can be heard: 'it' speaks there where 'I' have lost control.

The *Wake* is a continuous lapsus. It declares itself to be the 'lapse not leashed' (63.24) and it is the mechanism of the lapsus which allows the work to progress. The lapse is that moment in the world of communication when another subject speaks to another addressee across the phonetic and semantic levels of language. The lapse reveals us in our discourse and out of position, not placed in the comforting 'I' but displaced in the wake of our progress through language. Thus *Finnegans Wake* hesitates between a minimal control which takes us from line to line and a riot of meanings which invoke relations along a heterogeneous set of levels (phonetic, semantic, inter-linguistic). One consequence of recognising the importance of the lapsus is that it implies that *Finnegans Wake* is written in *English*. The answer to the question 'Are we speachin d'anglas landadge' (485.12/13) must be 'yes' because if there was not some continuity within the text then the lapsus would be impossible. It is necessary that we follow both the syntax and the major semantic concerns of any particular passage of the text lest it become a simple collocation of letters which offers no initial opposition to our passage through it.

*Finnegans Wake* is 'nat language at any sinse of the word'

(83.12). Which is to say language which goes beyond meaning (sense) and time (since) in an attempt to understand and abolish the sin involved in language: the guilt inherent in the very act of speaking or writing. It is in the second section of Book 2 of *Finnegans Wake*, the Nightlessons of the children, that we find this concern pushed to the very limit. This section caused Joyce almost more trouble than any other and he was forced, most unusually, to abandon some of the material that he wished to use. 'The Muddest Thick That Was Ever Heard Dump' was the initial title that Joyce gave to the geometry lesson and it is the geometry lesson which provides the central focus of the kaleidoscope of the book. Nightlessons of a 'nightynovel' (54.21), they are the essentials of the NIGHTLETTER (308.20). It is the section where Dolph, the Shem figure, describes to Kev, the Shaun figure, what is underneath the mother ALP's skirts. Kev secure in a male narcissism thinks that the results will be 'like pah' and 'as plane as a poke stiff' (296.28/30); he refuses to accept the possibility of difference. For it is at the moment that such a difference is accepted that the father ceases to be a full presence as he is articulated in the nets of difference.

What Joyce demonstrates in this section is that it is the phallus which is the determining term within the symbolic order and that it is the acceptance of this term which is crucial in the access to language and writing. It must be re-emphasised that the phallus must not be confused with the penis – the anatomical reality – but must be understood as the signifier of sexual difference, the possibility of the presence or absence of the object. It is with this possibility that the father becomes a term within the symbolic order, that the name becomes separated from the bearer. But if this rupture guarantees language, it is constantly annealed in the exigencies of communication, exigencies of meaning and identity. How far the claims of sense repress the movement of difference is determined by the social possibilities. Within *Finnegans Wake* it is nationalist politics which serves as the constant image of a new secure position for the subject from which the trauma of difference can be ignored. Kev can disavow what he has seen beneath the mother's skirts by fixing on another model of a full presence: on the heroic struggle for national liberation. But Dolph is intent on driving home the lessons of difference and of the secrets of writing. He urges Kev to 'pose the pen, man, way me does' (303.2/3) for the activity of writing will allow him to see that 'This is brave Danny weeping his spache for the popers. This is cool Connolly wiping his hearth with brave Danny. And this regard! how Chawleses Skewered parpara parnelligoes between brave Danny boy and the Connolly. Upanishadem! Top. Spoken hath L'arty Magory. Eregobragh. Prouf!' (303.8/14)

It is at this moment, as Dolph ridicules the three great heroes of Irish nationalism: Daniel O'Connell, Charles Ṣtewart Parnell and James Connolly, that Kev finally attacks his brother and knocks him down. To take up the position of writing, to allow absence to make itself felt is unthinkable for him. At all costs meaning and the father must be preserved against the onslaughts of Dolph, against the mocking of *Erin Go Bragh*. The proof that Dolph outlines is that the mother reveals the insufficiency of the father. It is this insufficiency that Kev cannot support and when the refuge that he has taken in nationalism and its heroes is threatened with dissolution by writing, he reacts in the only way possible – with violence. The mechanisms at work here are the same as those at work in the Cyclops episode when the Citizen attacks Bloom. Confronted with the reality of difference and the impossibility of definition (Bloom is both Irishman and Jew, the name is separated from the bearer), the secure ego reacts with violence. The threat of displacement must be resisted.

To speak is to have accepted a symbolic castration; to have accepted difference and absence. To enter into language is thus to have denied to the father his self-sufficiency and it is this denial which constitutes the guilt associated with language. The Shauns attempt to disavow this guilt and to concentrate simply on language as meaning but are thus excluded from the world of desire and writing; the Shems wallow in the guilt, become 'Shame's Voice' (one of Joyce's pseudonyms) but are exiled from the world of communication. If only Shem can write the letter, only Shaun can deliver it. The two are different elements of the same structure and it is for this reason that one can turn so easily into the other throughout the text. System is always likely to solidify into the position it upholds and position is constantly threatening to dissolve into the system that upholds it. The dissolution of Shaun in 111.iii provides an enactment of this process.

The *Wake* makes of the father only a name as he is 'variously catalogued, regularly regrouped' (129.12) in a play of language that turns him into a set of 'normative letters' (32.18) such that he becomes an 'apersonal problem, a locative enigma' (135.26/27). We are no longer engaged in a search for *the* father, for an origin, but in a study of the 'paradigmatic ear' (70.36) which is the place produced for the father by our forms of address, by our orders of discourse. One of the major metaphors for that place is Howth head. The mountain remains unchanged as the water takes its different forms around it: river, sea, vapour, rain. If the 'masculine monosyllables' (190.35) serve as the fixed point around which the rhythm flows, it is the feminine stream which provides the movement. Language is a constant struggle between a 'feminine libido' which threatens to break all boundaries and a 'male fist' which threatens to fix everything in place:

> . . . who thus at all this marvelling but will press on hotly to see the vaulting feminine libido of those interbranching ogham sex upandinsweeps sternly controlled and easily repersuaded by the uniform matteroffactness of a meandering male fist (123.06/9).

Anna Livia breaks with all forms of law be they secular or religious (139.25/28) but in so far as language depends on law, on a series of exclusions and oppositions, Anna cannot use language; she cannot write down her secrets. Symmetrically Shaun, who is the law-giver and embodies the law, is so fixed by its oppositions that he cannot create enough movement to let the symbols operate. For him, letters are 'tame, deep and

harried, in my mine's I' (425.25) and the consequences of his
ego's dominance of language is that, despite all his protests in
111.i, he cannot read the letter. If Anna Livia refuses to pay the
necessary attention to sexual difference which would enable her
to write, Shaun attempts to identify himself with the phallus, to
make himself a 'letter potent' (419.24) as a means of avoiding
the recognition that his brother has insisted on. Shaun's strategy of disavowal banishes him from the world of writing. Carried along by the river, he ignores its flow and thinks himself the
master of his own destiny. It is Shem who provides the point of
intersection between the male and female which allows the
possibility of writing. It is Anna Livia's tones that break
through Mercius' speech and it is Shem's ability to articulate
the mother's voice which is his ability to make the 'dumb speak'
(195.5).

Through its constant demonstration of the differences and
absences with which language is constituted, writing allows a
constant openness to the feminine. *Finnegans Wake* lets the unconscious speak by investigating the very act of writing; it tells
us the mother's secrets. But the mother speaks only in the position of the male, of the son, and in *Finnegans Wake* there is the
suggestion of another discourse which would find the mother
speaking through the daughter. Joyce's last text suggests that
there are two fundamentally different attitudes to language
which are articulated along sexual divisions. But this suggestion brings us to the limits of both *Finnegans Wake* and this book.
So far I have been content with explaining how Joyce's writing
breaks with that relation between the subject and language
which is exemplified by Shaun. The question of the other relation to language has been defined negatively in terms of this
'normal' relation. *Finnegans Wake* demands, however, a more
positive definition for it suggests that there is a totally different
attitude to language which can be characterised as female.

Within the text Issy, the daughter, functions as an insistent
reminder of a different attitude to language. During the Nightlessons she regards the twins' struggles as an irrelevance. While
the 'jemmijohns' will cudgel each other, she will not give a

damn ('her tootpettypout of jemenfichue') because she has had an opportunity of studying 'gramma's grammer (26807/17). Grandma's grammar insists on the dialogic basis to language and draws attention to the consequent reflexivity of both language and desire which makes of 'mind your genderous' an appropriate warning to anyone who attempts to speak (268.17/29). It is the lack of the knowledge of grandma's grammar which leaves the twins obsessed by the independent Cartesian ego – Kev wallowing in it and Dolph/Jerry attempting to write his way out of it (304.31). Grandma's grammar serves as the term to distinguish a language in which the experience of loss and absence is not determined by the reaction to sexual difference; a relation to the experiences of absence and loss which finds no unification in the articulation of the phallus. In an attempt to indicate what such a language and such an experience might be, a final reflection on the entry to the world of the symbol, of language, is necessary. This reflection must, however, be offered tentatively because the attempt to analyse Grandma's grammar takes us beyond the contemporary limits of psycho-analysis. Freud himself recognised these limits when, at the end of his life, he posed the famous question 'What does a woman want?' Here Joyce's practice remains in excess of any theoretical development. Here Joyce is still writing in our future.

I have attempted to explain how it is a submission to a central lack in being, a gap in the letter, that is the condition of the existence of desire and language. While, in an original moment, an identity of being is presumed, the correlation of alternative states of being with certain sounds entails the recognition of a set of differences which, from the undifferentiated world of being, pluck an object. The object is immediately already a possible absence, a lack in being, and its correlation with any given word depends on a set of differential relationships rather than on some divinely ordered one-to-one correspondence. The indeterminacy of these differential relationships (there are always more words, the system is inherently unstable) is what ensures that the letter has a gap in it, even in the moment of its discovery. This process of separation, which constitutes word and world in the same movement, is constant throughout the small child's life but it is the phallus which takes up metaphorically all these previous separations and thus becomes the privileged signifier, the key term around which all differential oppositions function. It is in terms of certain relations to the phallus that we can understand the terms of the entry of the subject (an entry which is its constitution) into language and desire.

The central role of the phallus is not determined by anatomical difference but by the way that the child understands it to be articulated within the mother's own desire, the evidence of her submission to the world of difference and language. It is thus the maternal grandfather who is the determining term in the child's entry into the symbolic. However, behind the mother's relation to the maternal grandfather, there rests her attachment to her own mother – the maternal grandmother. It is in the availability of the relation to the maternal grandmother that we might try to sketch the central differences in the formation of the male and female unconscious. These differences, which find no explanation within psycho-analytic theory, are, I believe, essential to any explanation of the language of *Finnegans Wake* which affords to the text the importance it deserves.

Joyce indicates that 'gramma's grammer' is available to girls but not to boys. This assymetry can be explicated in psycho-analytical terms by the fact that before the little girl can take up her symmetrical Oedipal relation with her father, she must separate herself from her mother. In one of his last attempts to deal with this problem, the essay entitled 'On Female Sexuality', Freud wrote of this first relation to the mother in the following despairing terms:

> Everything in the sphere of this first attachment to the mother seemed so difficult to grasp in analysis – so grey with age and shadowy and almost impossible to revivify – that it was as if it had succumbed to an especially inexorable repression (Freud 1931b, 21:226).

Some reflection on this first attachment and separation should convince us that it is impossible for the phallus to take up previous separations for the little girl in the same way that it does for the little boy. In the separation from the mother the small boy suffers a fundamental wound to his narcissism, a wound which ensures access to language but also a defence against the recognition of this wound. This double action results in a relation to language which we have seen exemplified in such as Buck Mulligan. The little girl's separation from the mother receives no such single determination. While the recognition of sexual difference must eventually function as the recognition of a possible loss, the little girl's first reaction is Issy's 'Funny spot to have a fingey!' (144.35). It is only after the little girl has taken up a position as inferior that the phallus can come to occupy the central symbolic position. What is important to notice is that in so far as the little girl's first identification proves correct, her narcissism is fundamentally different from the male's. Shaun's narcissism is always a defence involving aggression. Issy, like Alice, just looks in the mirror. But in so far as this fundamental narcissism is not challenged so the girl's grasp of language is not so sure, for there is no one term which takes up and stabilises the separations. One might ask what kind of discourse this organisation would produce and the answer might well be *Finnegans Wake*. Or, rather, it is the impact of this discourse on the phallocentric male discourse which produces *Finnegans Wake*. These alternatives present a difficult problem. Can we categorise the text as a feminine discourse despite its articulation by a male pen or must that pen be accounted for? The answer provided by psycho-analysis is ambiguous. On the one hand we have Freud's theory of bisexuality in which every position already implies every other and male and female confront one another as the constantly dividing term of an infinite regress. On this view any specific feature of the female constitution is always already inscribed in the male. On the other hand one might recall Freud's famous comment that 'Anatomy is Destiny' which, in its very phraseology, might seem to

allow an effectivity to the body over and above the representations it receives in the symbolic world. These two positions may
not in fact be incompatible. If we temporalise the process then
we can postulate that every new term will include the features of
the preceding terms but also features specific to itself which will
be passed on to further terms in the series. This solution has the
advantage of ensuring that the infinite regress cannot be translated into imaginary unities. It has the further advantage that it
squares with what we know of the construction of *Finnegans
Wake*. The original draft of the Nightlessons section was abandoned after much agony and its content scattered through the
final version as Issy's footnotes. The attempt to render Issy's
voice defeats Joyce who must rest content with speaking the
mother through the pen of Shem.

If we lack the theoretical concepts needed to develop these
considerations fully, we can say that in the *Wake* the women
function as the constant excess of any limits prescribed by the
male and an excess which demonstrates those limits as limits.
For the father the daughter embodies the last possibility of a
being who will believe in him as cause of his own desire. As
Anna Livia drifts towards death she remembers her husband's
wish for a daughter, 'What wouldn't you give to have a girl!'
(620.26/7) But the mother reveals the father's inadequacy as
she spells out 'my yearns to her' (620.36) because this lesson destroys the myth of the father's omnipotence. Anna Livia gets
the opportunity to instruct her daughter when the father has
taken the son out fishing and is impressing him by spinning
'yarns to him on the swishbarque waves' (620.35). The oppositions posed her provide a resumé of Joyce's themes: 'If you
spun your yarns to him on the swishbarque waves I was spelling
my yearns to her over cottage cake.' On the one hand you have
the story-telling father promising identity and position and on
the other you have the mother dividing language into its con-
stituent parts to let desire speak. Into the oppositions male and
female, position and desire *Finnegans Wake* introduces writing:
desire in position and position in desire, an ineradicable and
inexhaustible bisexuality, a constant process, 'The seim anew'

(215.23).

This acceptance of movement and process, coupled with the awareness of identity as a constant effect of the passage of language, has profound political implications for a society based on a notion of the individual as an independent and self-sufficient entity. It is only by the acceptance of the most reductive account of the relation between politics and literature that Joyce's texts can be dismissed as non-political. Traditionally we are accustomed to understand questions concerning the political nature of literature in terms of the specific political positions that are espoused or rejected within a work. But Joyce's writing renders such a criterion obsolete. Given the refusal of any hierarchy of discourses within a text, the political discourses inscribed within it lack any of those determinations which would enable the reader to correlate them as true or false against a given reality. Of course, the temptation may be to read them within the framework of classical irony and to presume that we are merely being shown the emptiness of all politics. Such a strategy of reading, however, must rely on the existence of a meta-language which Joyce's texts refuse. A refusal which can be read throughout his texts but particularly in the Cyclops section of *Ulysses* and 'Ivy Day in the Committee Room'.

Rather than engaging in the direct espousal of political positions, Joyce's work poses new questions about the relation between reader and text in ways that I have attempted to explicate. What remains to be discussed is the politics of this relation and the consequences of a practice of writing which subverts traditional political discourse. I have suggested that the crucial difference for the reader of Joyce lies in the position allocated him or her by the text. Instead of a traditional organisation of discourses which confer an imaginary unity on the reader, there is a disruption of any such position of unity. The reader is transformed into a set of contradictory discourses, engaged in the investigation of his or her own symbolic construction. What is subverted in the writing is the full Cartesian subject and this subversion is a political event of central importance. For with the loss of the punctual subject, it is no longer possible to indicate discrete areas in which the punctual subject is represented. Instead one is confronted with the problem of understanding the individual as a set of over-lapping and contradictory practices which produce a plurality of contradictory subjects. To understand the subject as plural and contradictory is to abandon a conception of politics as a de-terminate area with its specific discourses and organisation. When Lenin called for a 'new kind of party', he was challenging the assumption that those who wished to transform social re-lations could organise in a discrete area called 'politics'. Lenin's emphasis on 'style of work' and on 'self-criticism' can be understood as an attempt to find an organisational structure which would allow for the articulation of other practices within the area of representational politics and vice versa. The fact that the history of Leninist organisations is all too often the his-tory of the total subordination of other practices to the political (and the political understood in the narrowest of bourgeois senses) should not obscure the revolutionary nature of Lenin's call. And it is in terms of the desire for 'a new kind of party' that one can understand Joyce's texts as revolutionary in their com-mitment to the overthrow of the possibility of contemporary (both his and still ours) political discourse. Though it is also important to explain the relation between their subversive force and their profound political ineffectiveness.

To understand this contradiction it is necessary to consider the relation between form and politics. It is obvious that Joyce's texts produce a multitude of breaks with previous literary forms and in this book I hope to have demonstrated that these breaks can be articulated in terms of the allocation of contradictory positions to the reading subject. Crucial to this process is the production of a separation between the signifier and the signi-fied and the consequent de-naturalisation of signification. But in so far as one makes a merely formal claim for separation it would seem that the ideal text would be a simple collocation of letters. Such an abstract formalism is untenable and it is through a consideration of the lapsus that one can theorise the necessity for the text to produce enough unity for the separation to be effective as process. For in so far as the text remains totally resistant to any practices of reading it can only be experienced as boredom; it is the extent to which a text subverts a practice from within that it submits the reader to the experience of separation.

It is to Brecht, for whom form and politics were indissolubly linked, that we must return in order to understand the politics of separation within a text. Brecht's calls for an epic theatre were above all calls to break the unity that works of art conferred upon the spectator and to transform the passive consumption of meanings into the active appropriation of knowledge. Rather than a text compact with its own meaning, a text which confers a unity and gives a position to the subject, Brecht demands a text whose fissures and differences constantly force an activity of articulation on the subject; an articulation which in its constant changes and contradictions makes known, demonstrates, the contradictions of the reader's position both as reader and, in consequence, as agent in the world. But in order to achieve this work of separation (the work that *Finnegans Wake* constantly forces on us) it is necessary to begin where there is an identity. If we think back on those constitutive moments which produce us as sexed human beings then we can recognise a regularity whereby each psychic stage is the transformation of an identity – with the breast, the faeces, the phallus – into a separation. What is remarkable about each of these transformations is that they involve the fall from pleasure into desire and from belief to knowledge. For in so far as there is unity and identity the subject is a founding source, secure in its own self-sufficiency. The production of an object defined through its differences changes all this. For it allows both the possibility of knowledge (the studying of sets of differences which find their determination independently of their relation to the subject) and the possibility of desire because the object (in the very fact of its recognition) becomes a possible absence. It is this possibility of absence that condemns us forever to a world of unfulfilled desire because there can be no total enjoyment of an object.

Consciousness, however, is irrevocably bound up with a world of belief in which subject and object merge in intentionality. In so far as the object exists for consciousness it has been plucked forth from the undifferentiated mass of existence; it is defined through a set of differences. But consciousness, in its concern to maintain life, must studiously ignore this set of differences which are the conditions of the object's existence. Freud's discovery of the unconscious was formulated in terms of this contradiction when he recognised that the defining chain of differences constantly threatens to break and disrupt the necessarily homogeneous world of consciousness. Caught in the homogeneous state of consciousness, the object finds itself trapped in a unity of belief, conferred an identity. In order for there to be knowledge, there must be separation so that an identity can be displaced into its constitutive relationships. On the one hand we find identity and there we discover pleasure and belief and, on the other, we can produce separation and there we will find desire and knowledge.

The political question becomes the question of locating the identity which can be dissolved and appropriated as knowledge. The concept which enables us to pose this question is the central concept of epic theatre – the gest. Benjamin, writing of epic theatre, defined the gest in terms of interruption, the freezing of a moment so that an imaginary vision of obviousness is replaced by a set of relationships to be examined:

The damming of the stream of life, the moment when its flow comes to a standstill, makes itself felt as reflux: this reflux is astonishment. . . . But if the stream of things breaks against this rock of astonishment, then there is no difference between a human life and a word. In epic theatre both are only the crest of the wave. Epic theatre makes life spurt up high from the bed of time and, for an instant, hover irridescent in empty space. Then it puts it back to bed (Benjamin 1973b, p. 13).

Benjamin's characterisation of a word and a human life as

the same for epic theatre serves to emphasise that epic theatre breaks with that identity given to a life in the course of experience, or a word in the flow of speech, in order to make clear that their identity can only be defined through a set of differences – the relationships that define them. The gest, then, is a set of relationships revealed by an interruption and one can see how usefully this concept could be used to characterise Joyce's work where it is often a question of interruptions which reveal a set of relationships (one could use the gest to define the structure of *Dubliners*). But in order for astonishment to be generated it is necessary that an obvious identity must subsume the relationships which are revealed by the interruption. In other words it is only when the world of pleasure and belief is interrupted that desire and knowledge become possible. The starting point must always be a recognised identity.

We can now understand how the political question for any specific text is not whether the text 'contains' the correct political line as part of its content but whether it addresses a specific identity or identities and whether it confirms these identities in an imaginary exchange or whether it transforms them into a network of relations which thus become available for knowledge and action. In so far as any individual is a contradictory set of these imaginary identities, it is not a question of addressing an individual in his or her totality but of isolating one of those images, that of husband or wife, mother or son, intellectual or worker, and attempting, by means of that action of 'freezing' which Benjamin describes, to demonstrate that identity as a set of social relations, a demonstration which does not take place either *in* the text or *in* the reader's head but in the active relation between both. The political question to be posed in relation to Joyce's texts is whether the constant fragmentation of the imaginary is determined in terms of particular identities. If the question is asked in these terms then an answer will necessarily include an analysis of a particular political situation.

Considerations like these make it evident that Joyce's texts are politically ineffective because they lack any definite notion of the audience to which they are addressed. It is obvious from

Joyce's disappointment at the reaction to *Ulysses* and *Finnegans Wake* that he entertained some notion of the common reader to whom his texts would be available. But this purely imaginary audience did not exist and the real audience to whom the texts are thus necessarily addressed is an isolated individual and the only possible individual: Joyce himself. It is this resurrection of the notion of the individual at the limit of texts dedicated to the subversion of that notion which has allowed Joyce to be so easily recuperated by literary critics. In so far as Joyce addresses an individual he can be read as an investigator of an essential human nature and this reading can find further evidence in his use of theorists like Vico and Bruno. It is important to stress both that Joyce's practice of writing moves beyond any notion of an immutable individual human nature to investigate the very processes of that nature's variable construction *and* that the fact that he is the only audience inscribed in the text resurrects that immutable and individual human nature. If the effort of reading Brecht or Eisenstein is the effort of understanding the political conjunctures in which their texts were produced (and many of the elements in those conjunctures remain contemporary), the effort of reading Joyce is one of imaginary identification. In order to place ourselves in the position from which the processes of separation in *Finnegans Wake* can be experienced, it is necessary to have a commitment to Joyce. The only section of society that shares an imaginary identity with Joyce are the Joyce scholars and it is they who form his only audience.[1]

---

[1] In another context it might be necessary to draw distinctions between the different sections of this audience, for example between the professional and amateur Joyce scholars. However, what is important for the general political argument is that Joyce's audience do not share a political or social identity which is figured centrally in the text.

# 7

# Joyce's Politics

It would be easy to upbraid Joyce for his failure to address a
specific audience but so to do is to indulge in the easy moralism
of political commitment. The important task is to attempt to
understand the political and historical reasons for this failure
rather than to produce the sterile condemnation of an individual. And such a task is not only difficult but painful as its
necessary starting-point is the acknowledgement of the failures
of socialism in twentieth-century Europe. It can be argued that
socialism failed in 1914 when the social-democratic parties
rallied to the chauvinist standards of the various national
powers. This failure reveals not merely, as Lenin would have it,
a misunderstanding of the logic of imperialism (and we shall
see that this Leninist position avoids many of the problems),
but more particularly the failure of the parties of the Second
International to confront and analyse those elements of politics
that are not reducible to a rational conflict of interests. For in
politics it is not simply interests but imaginary identities which
are at stake. Identifications with particular ideological discourses (my country, my faith) may replace the earlier and
inevitably disappointing identification with the father. The
displacement of these identifications involves more than is provided by a rational discourse about interests or by the offer to
replace country and faith by international brotherhood. If we
consider the capitulation of social democracy to be the result of
a conception of politics which refused to take the problems of

identification as vital then it could be argued that the Third International was just as much an heir of the 'betrayal' of 1914 as the Second.[1]

It is little realised, and never stressed, that Joyce's life before 1914 gave him the very rare opportunity to observe two of the most important political developments of the twentieth century. If the three great political themes of the nineteenth century had been democracy, socialism and nationalism, the twentieth century saw three movements constitute themselves around these themes: anti-colonialism, Communism and Fascism. After the fall of Parnell, Ireland witnessed a general disenchantment with parliamentary politics that made the Dublin of Joyce's youth the breeding-ground for the Easter Rising. In the shift from Parnell, the parliamentary leader (albeit unorthodox), to Pearse and Connolly, the armed insurrectionists, we move from a classic nineteenth-century nationalist movement to a struggle which finds its analogues in those other anti-colonial guerrilla wars which have punctuated our century. The union of bourgeois nationalism and proletarian socialism which gave birth to the Irish Republican Army has become familiar to us in a host of national liberation movements.

Joyce's travels in Europe also provided him with important political experience. The Trieste in which he argued for socialism against the ultra-nationalist Irredentists became, five years after he left it, the first Fascist city in Europe:

During the first half of 1920 the new fascist movement remained a circumscribed phenomenon of little importance. The only Italian city it succeeded in penetrating was Trieste, whose atmosphere was in many ways exceptional: the closeness of Fiume, the military administration to which the city was subjected, and above all the existence of a state of

[1] As was suggested in Chapter 6, many of the practices of the Bolshevik party in Russia were very effective in combating the repressive identifications of nationalism. However, in the absence of a theory of these practices, there was no possibility of systematically elaborating appropriate practices in different situations. Indeed the working class movement has often been hampered by the imaginary ideal of a 'Bolshevik party'.

chronic tension between Slav and Italian populations, which had been greatly aggravated by the end of Austrian rule, made Trieste a good breeding-ground for an intensely nationalistic movement such as Fascism (Procacci 1973, pp. 415–16).

The major component in both the embryonic movements in whose gestation Joyce participated was nationalism and it is nationalism, and in particular Irish nationalism, that dominates both the political writings of the pre-First World War period (letters, articles and lectures) and the political concerns of his later texts. But in the early period, and especially in the letters to Stanislaus written between 1905 and 1907, there is another political component: revolutionary socialism. In these letters we can read the contradiction between an optimism engendered by Italian socialist politics and a pessimism confirmed by the developments of Irish nationalism. Joyce's politics were largely determined by attitudes to sexuality. Central to his commitment to socialism was his ferocious opposition to the institution of marriage, bourgeois society's sanctified disavowal of the reality of desire:

It is a mistake for you to imagine that my political opinions are those of a universal lover: but they are those of a socialistic artist. I cannot tell you how strange I feel sometimes in my attempt to live a more civilised life than my contemporaries. But why should I have brought Nora to a priest or a lawyer to make her swear away her life to me? And why should I superimpose on my child the very troublesome burden of belief which my father and mother superimposed on me (letter to Stanislaus Joyce, 2 or 3 May 1905)?

Joyce's hatred of the institution of marriage was paralleled by his dislike for the form of parliamentary democracy. His desire for a complete break with the repressive fabric of bourgeois society made him a natural supporter of anarchosyndicalism, at that time the most revolutionary faction in the Italian Socialist Party. The P.S.I. Congress of 1906, which

Joyce followed closely, saw four tendencies competing for control of the Party. The major disagreement was between the traditional reformist wing of the Party whose policy involved alliance with the anti-clerical and radical bourgeois Parties in Parliament and the syndicalists who argued that nothing was to be gained from participation in a bourgeois institution. This major argument was complicated by a Marxist faction which stood for participation in Parliament but a refusal of any alliance with bourgeois Parties and a group known as the Integralists (an ideology peculiar to Italian politics) which adopted the line that the other three tendencies were partially correct and that elements of all three strategies should be incorporated in the party platform. Joyce, who had already signalled his interest in the leader of the syndicalists, was in no doubt where his sympathies lay:

I am following with interest the struggle between the various socialist parties here at the Congress: Labriola spoke yesterday, the paper says, with extraordinary rapid eloquence for two hours and a half. He reminds me somewhat of Griffith. He attacked the intellectual and the parliamentary socialists. He belongs to or is the leader of the sindicalists. They are trades-unionists or rather trade-unionists with a definite anti-social programme. Their weapons are unions and strikes. They decline to interfere in politics or religion or legal questions. They do not desire the conquest of public powers, which, they say, only serve in the end to support the middle-class government. They assert they are true socialists because they wish the future social order to proceed equally from the overthrow of the entire present social organisation and from the automatic emergence of the proletariat in trades-unions and guilds and the like. Their objection to parliamentarianism seems to me well-founded but if, as all classes of socialists agree, a general European war, an international war, has become an impossibility I do not see how a general international strike or even a national strike is a possibility. The Italian army is not directed against the

Austrian army so much as against the Italian people. Of
course, the sindicalists are anti-militarists but I don't see
how that saves them from the logical conclusion of revolution
in a conscriptive country like this (letter to Stanislaus Joyce,
9 October 1906).

So enthusiastic was Joyce about syndicalism that he even
used the political strike as a metaphor for his own literary practice:

If it is not far-fetched to say that my action, and that of men
like Ibsen & c, is a virtual intellectual strike I would call such
people as Gogarty and Yeats and Colm the blacklegs of
literature. Because they have tried to substitute us, to serve
the old idols at a lower rate when we refused to do so for a
higher (letter to Stanislaus Joyce, 6 November 1906).

His interest in Italian politics also supplied him with some
theoretical basis for his support for Griffith's movement which
called for both political and economic independence for Ireland:

You ask me what I would substitute for parliamentary agi-
tation in Ireland. I think the *Sinn Fein* policy would be more
effective. Of course I see that its success would be to substitute Irish for English capital but no one, I suppose, denies
that capitalism is a stage of progress. The Irish proletariat
has yet to be created. A feudal peasantry exists, scraping the
soil but this would with a national revival or with a definite
preponderance of England surely disappear. I quite agree
with you that Griffith is afraid of the priests – and he has
every reason to be so. But, possibly, they are also a little
afraid of him too. After all he is holding out some secular
liberty to the people and the Church doesn't approve of that.
I quite see, of course, that the Church is still, as it was in the
time of Adrian IV, the enemy of Ireland, but I think her time
is almost up. For either *Sinn Fein* or Imperialism will conquer

the present Ireland. If the Irish programme did not insist on the Irish language I suppose I could call myself a nationalist. As it is, I am content to recognise myself an exile: and, prophetically, a repudiated one (letter to Stanislaus Joyce, 6 November 1906).

If these views occurred without contradiction then one might be forgiven for describing Joyce in 1906 as a potential convert to Leninism. His support for the syndicalist programme tempered by his scepticism about the frailty of the bourgeois state placed him in the company of many who argued on the side of the Leninist faction in the Second International before 1914.

But there is another set of political concerns in these letters and they run counter to the easy optimism that the Church's influence would be destroyed by social changes. For Joyce was all too well aware that the power of the Church was grounded in a repressive order of sexuality which could survive and negate 'inevitable' social change. Any revolution would have to address itself to these problems if it were to result in any significant liberation. This necessity can be seen in Joyce's violent reaction to the news of Gogarty's marriage. To participate in such an institution was to perpetuate a reactionary order which controlled the political as well as the sexual sphere, as he made clear in a letter to Stanislaus:

> You have often shown opposition to my socialistic tendencies. But can you not see plainly from facts like these [Gogarty's marriage] that a deferment of the emancipation of the proletariat, a reaction to clericalism or aristocracy or bourgeoisism would mean a revulsion to tyrannies of all kinds? Gogarty would jump in the Liffey to save a man's life but he seems to have little hesitation in condemning generations to servitude. . . . For my part I believe that to establish the church in full power again in Europe would mean a renewal of the Inquisition . . . (letter to Stanislaus Joyce, about 12 August 1906).

The connection between repressed desire and nationalism was insisted on by Joyce in his comments on an article which Gogarty had published in Griffith's paper. Gogarty had condemned the English for their sexual habits and had accused them of being riddled with venereal disease. Joyce told Stanislaus:

> What I object to most of all in his [Griffith's] paper is that it is educating the people of Ireland on the old pap of racial hatred whereas anyone can see that if the Irish question exists, it exists for the Irish proletariat chiefly. I have expressed myself badly, I fear, but perhaps you will be able to get at what I mean (letter to Stanislaus Joyce, 25 September 1906).

Joyce's difficulties of expression (almost unparalleled in his letters) are not fortuitous. The theoretical articulation of the relation between politics and sexuality and the particular nature of nationalist ideologies defy socialists today as they did seventy years ago. If we are any nearer to understanding the processes at work in nationalism, it is in large measure due to Joyce's own investigation of these relations, an investigation which eschewed theory in favour of a practice of writing which would exhibit and displace the repressive nature of nationalist discourse. At the level of theory, Joyce was reduced to impotent paroxysms of rage by *Sinn Fein*'s continued campaign against the 'venereal excess' of the English:

> I am nauseated by their lying drivel about pure men and pure women and spiritual love and love for ever: blatant lying in the face of truth. I don't know very much about the 'saince' of the subject but I presume there are very few mortals in Europe who are not in danger of waking some morning and finding themselves syphilitic. (letter to Stanislaus Joyce, 13 November 1906).

Griffith's movement was destined to capitulate to these

repressive forces and Joyce's interest in Irish politics waned. When he lectured to the inhabitants of Trieste in April 1907 he declared: '. . . I confess that I do not see what good it does to fulminate against the English tyranny while the Roman tyranny occupies the palace of the soul' (CW 173).

Joyce's concern with the palace of the soul, Stephen Dedalus' desire to kill the priest and king within, are the result of the specific nature of Irish society and politics. But the problems that Joyce, as Irish, faced from his youth, were to openly dismay European socialism with the outbreak of war in 1914. The capitulation of the social-democratic parties, so evident in retrospect, was a thunderbolt at the time. Lenin quite simply refused to believe that the German S.P.D. had voted war credits and was convinced that the edition of *Vorwärts* that carried the news was a forgery. That the endless resolutions of the Second International, affirmed and re-affirmed over twenty-five years, could be proved worthless in four days, such a thought was, almost literally, unthinkable. While Lenin's theory of imperialism had predicted such a war as inevitable and whereas he had foreseen the ineffectiveness of the social-democratic parties to stop it, he had not foreseen their enthusiastic rush to the ranks of national defence. In August 1914 the working-class movement was confronted with a problem to which it has yet, over sixty years later, to provide a solution. Nor should it be thought that such a solution is simply a question of theory. It is probable that to deal with this problem would entail a more radical break with bourgeois forms of politics than any Western Socialist or Communist Party has yet attempted. For it would become necessary to combat at the level of organisation and style of work the forms of identification that binds us to our 'mother' or 'father' land,[1] those forms of identification which cause the sen-

[1] Whatever the gender, the image of the nation possesses a symbolic penis. This possession may be figured directly in the image of the phallic woman, familiar to us as Athena. France's 'Marianne' and England's 'Britannia' are just two of the many variations on that theme. Alternatively, the woman can be figured as a mother, but a mother whose only function is to produce sons, beings endowed with that object which will make her complete. Both images function as a denial of the reality of female desire.

sation of panic in grown men when 'the cry goes up that Throne and Altar are in danger'.

If forms of political practice would have to be altered, it is also clear that major theoretical developments would be involved. The Marxist tradition calls for political problems to be analysed in terms of the forces and relations of production, that is to say, in terms of the class struggle. Two movements have, however, consistently proved resistant to such analyses: nationalism and feminism. In both cases, Marxists have a history of opportunistic tactics without any clear strategy. Stalin's pamphlet on nationalism, written in 1913, continues to determine the terms of the debate within the Marxist tradition (despite the fact that its authorship determines that the pamphlet itself is never read). Stalin proposed a set of criteria to determine nationhood (amongst which notions of community, historical development and a shared language are crucial) and further held that any people who satisfied these criteria had the right to national self-determination. Recent critics have argued that there can be no abstract definition of nationhood and nationalism and that each specific set of nationalist demands must be understood in relation to the particular balance of class forces (cf. Terray 1973). Both positions avoid the heterogeneous reality of nationalism, on the one hand reducing it to a set of 'natural facts' and on the other reducing it to the class struggle. Instead one should talk of the conditions of existence for any nationalist movement, conditions which will include not only the criteria which Stalin enumerated *and* the state of the forces and relations of production *but also* the forms of representation within which the political demands are articulated, forms which will not be reducible to the state of the class struggle.[1] Only with this analysis is it possible to make the necessary

---

[1] Feminism is the only mass political movement which has constantly tried to analyse and combat those forms of representation and the identities they confer on us. If the working-class movement has time and again underestimated the dangers of nationalism, it has reciprocally failed to understand the importance of a real alliance with the feminist movement. Joyce, at least, had no doubts concerning the importance of feminism. Defending Ibsen to Arthur Power, he said 'As I say . . . you do not understand him. You ignore the spirit

discriminations. In so far as nationalism persists in 'familialis-ing' the relation of the individual to a community or to a State, persists in making us 'sons' or 'daughters' of the 'mother' or 'father' land then it must be combated. For it is in the pro-duction and reproduction of these relations (processes which are not simply a question of vocabulary) that we can locate the profoundly reactionary reality of nationalism. Such a nationalism confers identity and belief there where we would find desire and knowledge.

If we consider nationalism in this perspective then it is clear why Joyce was unable to address an audience in Ireland. For Joyce's lifetime witnesses, in the success of the Irish national revolution, the triumph of the most sexually repressive and politically reactionary form of nationalism. If, as Joyce had ear-lier believed, only socialism could give a progressive and liber-ating character to nationalist demands, then the years before 1914 seemed full of hope. The rapid growth of mass unionism under the leadership of Larkin and Connolly introduced a new force into Irish politics. When the strike of 1913 resulted in the formation of the Irish Citizen Army as the military wing of the trade unionist movement, it was not impossible that the work-ing class might wrest the leadership from the discredited parlia-mentary party and the revolutionary nationalists of the Irish Republican Brotherhood. But 1914 saw the end of these hopes. When Connolly heard the news that the Second International had failed, he immediately demanded to be put in touch with Pearse and the other leaders of the Irish Republican Brother-hood. Reading his speeches and articles before and after 1914 is to understand something of the debilitating effect of the Inter-national's failure to stop the war. Sean O'Casey, who resigned the secretaryship of the Irish Citizen Army because of its refusal to break with the nationalists, described Connolly's transfor-mation thus:

which animated him. The purpose of *The Doll's House*, for instance, was the emancipation of women, which has caused the greatest revolution in our time in the most important relationship there is – that between men and women; the revolt of women against the idea that they are the mere instruments of men' (Power 1974, p. 35).

It is difficult to understand the almost revolutionary change that was manifesting itself in Connolly's nature. The Labour movement seemed to be regarded by him as a decrescent force while the essence of Nationalism began to assume the finest elements of his nature. His articles that now appeared in the *Worker's Republic* with consistent regularity, the speeches that he delivered at various demonstrations and assemblies, all proclaimed that Jim Connolly had stepped from the narrow byway of Irish socialism onto the broad and crowded highway of Irish Nationalism. The vision of the suffering world's humanity was shadowed by the nearer oppression of his own people, and in a few brief months pressed into a hidden corner of his soul the accumulated thoughts of a lifetime and opened his broad heart to ideas that altered the entire trend of his being. The high creed of Irish Nationalism became his daily rosary, while the higher creed of international humanity that had so long bubbled from his eloquent lips was silent for ever, and Irish Labour lost a leader.

A well-known author has declared that Connolly was the first martyr for Irish Socialism; but Connolly was no more an Irish Socialist martyr than Robert Emmett, P. H. Pearse or Theobald Wolfe Tone (O'Casey 1919, p. 52).

Of course, O'Casey's views have been bitterly contested by others in the Irish Labour movement. In his biography of Connolly, Greaves argues persuasively for the strategic necessity of uniting the national and social struggles, but one can concede that (as O'Casey and Joyce did) and yet argue that the form of that union was disastrous. Our analysis has indicated the importance of the forms of identification involved in any nationalist movement. It was Connolly's acceptance of the most reactionary and repressive of these forms that was catastrophic for the working-class movement in Ireland. Pearse's argument for the necessity of blood-sacrifice, the need for the sons to bleed for their mother Cathleen ni Houlihan in order to render the people worthy of nationhood, was enthusiastically taken up by Connolly. Arguing for such a sacrifice Connolly concluded an editorial in the *Irish Worker* of 5 February 1916 with the following words: 'Without the slightest trace of irreverence but in all due humility and awe, we recognise that of us, as of mankind before Calvary, it may be truly said "without the shedding of blood there is no redemption".'

It can be little cause for wonder that the union of the social and national struggles did not survive Connolly's death. There was no theoretical or ideological basis for the working class to involve themselves in the national struggle except by submitting to nationalist ideology. From 1916 onwards the representatives of the Irish labour movement refused to intervene in nationalist politics. The inevitable result was that the State that achieved independence in 1922 was to prove one of the most reactionary in Europe. Joyce's analysis of the situation, revealed in conversation with Arthur Power, was decidedly pessimistic:

In the Dublin of my day there was the kind of desperate freedom which comes from a lack of responsibility, for the English were in governance then, so everyone said what he liked. Now I hear that since the Free State came in there is less freedom. The Church has made inroads everywhere, so that we are in fact becoming a bourgeois nation, with the Church supplying the aristocracy . . . and I do not see much hope for us intellectually. Once the Church is in command she will devour everything . . . what she will leave will be a few old rags not worth the having: and we may degenerate to the position of a second Spain (Power 1974, p. 65).

Joyce's refusal to visit the Free State was based on sound political judgement. His conviction that he would be subjected to physical violence if he returned to Ireland was not, as most commentators will have it, the caprice of a mad artist but, as the briefest study of Irish independence demonstrates, a justified fear. Deprived of an audience that would allow his texts to function politically,[1] Joyce's writing becomes a more and more desperate attempt to deconstruct those forms of identification which had allowed the triumph of the national revolution to mean the very opposite of a liberation of Ireland.

The failure of the Irish revolution left Joyce no political debate in which he could participate. In order to talk he had to produce his own interlocuteurs. If one accepts the analysis of the role of the audience in determining the politics of a work of art then one must allow that no audience is available. The identities from which the artist must start to work may be too fixed to permit the construction of the experiments implied by Brecht's aesthetics. It may well be that art can only participate in a revolutionary politics. If such a politics does not exist then the writer is inevitably condemned to be 'apolitical', his or her political role reduced to a constant interrogation of the form of

[1] There was, of course, a period when Joyce did enjoy an audience which was more than a collection of individuals united only in their admiration of Joyce. During and after the first World War, and largely because of Pound's enthusiastic support, Joyce was an important figure in English literary circles. This English audience disappeared very quickly in the early 1920s (cf. Parrinder 1977). The reasons for Joyce's rejection are complex and they include the practical difficulty of obtaining Joyce's texts because of censorship. A full analysis would entail an account of the attitudes of intellectuals to politics from the moment that a working-class party became a significant presence in the 1890s. However, one can indicate that the rejection of Joyce was the product of a refusal to countenance the radical subversion which his writing entailed. Parrinder demonstrates that this refusal took symptomatic exception to Joyce's 'cloacal obsession'. The rejection of the materiality of the letter and anality as both subversive of an identity guaranteed by a fetishised penis can be read most clearly in the extraordinary letter which Pound sent Joyce on receiving the Sirens chapter. His dislike of the linguistic experimentation which he feels has gone too far is linked to an almost pathological reaction to Bloom's fart: 'gallic preference for Phallus – purely personal – know mittel europa humour runs to other orifice – But don't think you will strengthen your impact by that particular' (letter to James Joyce, 10 June 1919). Joyce obviously understood what was at stake in this rejection of The Sirens. Ten years later he wrote to Miss Weaver a propos of his own politics that 'the more I hear of the political, philosophical, ethical zeal and labours of the brilliant members of Pound's big brass band, the more I wonder why I was ever let into it "with my magic flute" (letter to Harriet Shaw Weaver, 22 November 1929). Joyce's opposition between the brass and wind section refers us back to The Sirens where Boylan's horn is opposed to Bloom's flute, the dominating phallus to the subversive anus.

politics. This is perhaps what Brecht meant when he wrote:

> The practical methods of the revolution are not revol-
> utionary, they are dictated by the class struggle. It is for this
> reason that great writers find themselves ill at ease in the
> class struggle, they behave as though the struggle was
> already finished, and they deal with the new situation, con-
> ceived as collectivist, which is the aim of the revolution. The
> revolution of the great writers is permanent (Brecht 1970,
> p. 25).

# Bibliography

This bibliography is divided into three. In each case the principle of selection is to include all relevant works referred to in the main body of the text together with uncited works which were essential to its composition. The first section deals with Joyce's own writings and the second with biographies and criticism of Joyce. Full bibliographies can be found in John J. Slocum and Herbert Cahoon, *A Bibliography of James Joyce 1882–1941* and Robert H. Deming, *A Bibliography of Joyce Studies*. These original bibliographical studies can be supplemented by the bibliographies in the *PMLA* and the additional details published in the *James Joyce Quarterly*. The third section contains all other material.

### SECTION 1    THE WRITINGS OF JAMES JOYCE

(A) WRITINGS PUBLISHED IN JOYCE'S LIFETIME
Note: Whatever edition is cited, the order of Joyce's texts follows the chronology of original publication.
'The Sisters', *Irish Homestead,* (Dublin, 13 August 1904) pp. 676–7. Published above the name Stephen Daedelus.
*Chamber Music* (London, 1907).
*Dubliners.* The Corrected Text, with an Explanatory Note by Robert Scholes, illustrated with fifteen drawings by Robin Jacques (London, 1967).
*A Portrait of the Artist as a Young Man.* The Definitive Text,

corrected from the Dublin Holograph by Chester G. Anderson and edited by Richard Ellmann (London, 1968).

*Exiles,* A Play in Three Acts, with the Author's Own Notes and an Introduction by Padraic Colum (London, 1952).

A first version of the Cyclops entitled simply 'Episode XII of *Ulysses*' appeared in *The Little Review,* vol. VI, no. 7, November 1919, pp. 38–54; no. 8, December 1919, pp. 50–60; no. 9, January 1920, pp. 53–61 and no. 10, March 1920, pp. 54–60.

*Ulysses* (London, 1960).

*Pomes Penyeach* (Paris, 1927).

*Finnegans Wake* (London, 1975).

(B) WRITINGS PUBLISHED AFTER JOYCE'S DEATH

Note: The order roughly corresponds to the times of original composition.

*Epiphanies,* edited by O. A. Silverman (Buffalo, 1956).

*The Critical Writings of James Joyce,* edited by Ellsworth Mason and Richard Ellmann (London, 1959).

*Stephen Hero,* edited by John J. Slocum, Herbert Cahoon and Theodore Spencer with a Foreword by John J. Slocum and Herbert Cahoon and an Introduction by Theodore Spencer and an Editorial Note (London, 1969).

*Giacomo Joyce,* edited with an Introduction and Notes by Richard Ellmann (London, 1968).

*James Joyce's Ulysses Notesheets in the British Museum,* edited by Phillip F. Herring (Charlottesville, 1972).

*James Joyce's Scribbledehobble: The Ur-Workbook for Finnegans Wake,* edited, with Notes and an Introduction, by Thomas E. Connolly (Chicago, 1961).

*A First Draft Version of Finnegans Wake,* edited and annotated by David Hayman (London, 1963).

*Anna Livia Plurabelle; The Making of a Chapter,* edited, with an Introduction, by F. H. Higginson (Minneapolis, 1960).

*Letters of James Joyce,* vol. 1. edited by Stuart Gilbert (London, 1957). Vols. 2 and 3, edited by Richard Ellmann (London, 1966).

SECTION 2    BIOGRAPHICAL AND CRITICAL
WORKS ON JAMES JOYCE

Adams, Robert M. (1962), *Surface and Symbol: The Consistency of James Joyce's ULYSSES.* New York.

Asenjo, F. G. (1964), 'The General Problem of Sentence Structure: An Analysis prompted by the loss of subject in *Finnegans Wake* in *Centennial Review of Arts and Sciences*, VIII, pp. 398–408.

Atherton, James S. (1959), *The Books at the Wake; a study of literary allusions in James Joyce's Finnegans Wake.* London.

Beckett, Samuel (1929), *et al. Our Exagmination Round his Factification for Incamination of Work in Progress.* Paris.

Budgen, Frank (1972), *James Joyce and the Making of Ulysses and other writings,* with an introduction by Clive Hart. Oxford.

Burgess, Anthony (1965), *Here Comes Everybody: an Introduction to James Joyce for the Ordinary Reader.* London.

—— (1973), *Joysprick: an Introduction to the Language of James Joyce.* London.

Byrne, J. F. (1953), *Silent Years: An Autobiography with Memoirs of James Joyce and Our Ireland.* New York.

Campbell, Joseph and Robinson, Henry M. (1944), *A Skeleton Key to Finnegans Wake.* London.

Carens, James F. (1972), 'Joyce and Gogarty' in *New Light on Joyce from the Dublin Symposium,* ed. Fritz Senn, Bloomington. pp. 28–45.

Cixous, Hélène (1964), *The Exile of James Joyce.* London, 1976.

—— (1970), 'Joyce, la ruse de l'écriture' in *Poétique*, no. 4, pp. 419–32.

Colum, Mary and Padraic (1959), *Our Friend James Joyce.* London.

Curran, C. P. (1968), *James Joyce Remembered.* Oxford.

Dahl, Lisa (1970), 'The Linguistic Presentation of the Interior Monologue in James Joyce's *Ulysses*' in *James Joyce Quarterly*, vol. 7, no. 2, pp. 114–20.

Deming, Robert H. (ed.) (1970), *James Joyce: The Critical Heritage*. 2 vols. London.

Ellmann, Richard (1966), *James Joyce*. Oxford.

—— (1977), *The Consciousness of Joyce*. London.

Gifford, Don and Seidman, Robert J. (1974), *Notes for Joyce: an annotation of James Joyce's Ulysses*. New York.

Gilbert, Stuart (1952), *James Joyce's Ulysses*. 2nd ed., revised. London.

Glasheen, Adaleen (1963), *A Second Census of Finnegans Wake*. London.

Golden, Sean V. (1974), 'The Kissier Licence: Liberty at the *Wake*' in *A Wake Newslitter* n.s. vol. XI, no. 5, pp. 79–84.

Hanley, Miles L. (1962), *Word Index to James Joyce's Ulysses*. Madison.

Hart, Clive (1962), *Structure and Motif in Finnegans Wake*. London.

—— (1963), *A Concordance to Finnegans Wake*. Minneapolis.

Hayman, David (1966), 'Scribbledehobbles and how they grew' in *Twelve and a Tilly*, edited by Jack P. Datton and Clive Hart. London, pp. 107–18.

Heath, Stephen (1972a), 'Ambiviolences: Notes pour la lecture de Joyce' in *Tel Quel*, no. 50, pp. 22–43 and *Tel Quel*, no. 51, pp. 64–77.

—— (1973), 'Trames de lecture' in *Tel Quel*, no. 54, pp. 4–15.

Herring, Phillip F. (1972), 'Joyce's Politics' in *New Light on Joyce from the Dublin Symposium*, edited by F. Senn, Bloomington, pp. 3–14.

Hodgart, M. J. C. and Worthington, M. P. (1959), *Song in the Works of James Joyce*. New York.

Joyce, Stanislaus (1958), *My Brother's Keeper*, edited by Richard Ellmann. London.

—— (1962), *The Dublin Diary of Stanislaus Joyce*, edited by George Harris Healey. London.

Kenner, Hugh (1974), 'Circe' in *James Joyce's Ulysses; Critical Essays*, edited by Clive Hart and David Hayman. Berkeley, pp. 341–62.

Leavis, F. R. (1933a), 'James Joyce and the Revolution of the

Word' in *Scrutiny,* vol. 2, no. 2, pp. 193–201.

Litz, A. Walton (1961), *The Art of James Joyce: Method and Design in Ulysses and Finnegans Wake*. London.

McDiarmid, Hugh (1955), *In memoriam James Joyce: from a Vision of World Language*. Glasgow.

Mercanton, Jacques (1968), *Les Heures de James Joyce*. Lausanne.

Norris, Margot (1977), *The Decentered Universe of Finnegans Wake; A Structuralist Analysis*. Baltimore.

Parrinder, Patrick (1977), 'The Strange Necessity: James Joyce's Rejection in England 1914–30' Unpublished Paper.

Pound, Ezra (1968), *Pound/Joyce; The Letters of Ezra Pound to James Joyce with Pound's Essays on Joyce,* edited and with commentary by Forrest Read, London.

Power, Arthur (1974), *Conversations with James Joyce,* edited by Clive Hart. London.

Purdy, Strother (1972), 'Mind Your Genderous: Toward a *Wake* Grammar' in *New Light on Joyce from the Dublin Symposium,* edited by Fritz Senn, Bloomington, pp. 46–78.

Rabaté, Jean-Michel (1976), 'Lapsus ex machina' in *Poétique* no. 26, pp. 152–72.

—— (1977), 'Bisexuality in *Finnegans Wake*: Bypasses of Desire and Bylaws of the Imaginary'. Unpublished Paper.

Schlauch, Margaret (1939), 'The Language of James Joyce' in *Science and Society,* vol. 3, pp. 482–97.

Senn, Fritz (1960), 'Every litty of a scolderymeid: Sexual-Political Analogies' in *A Wake Newslitter,* No. 3, pp. 1–7.

—— (1974), 'Nausicaa' in *James Joyce's Ulysses; Critical Essays,* edited by Clive Hart and David Hayman. Berkeley. pp. 277–312.

Silverstein, N. (1974), *Joyce's Circe Episode: Approaches to Ulysses through a Textual and Interpretative Study of Joyce's Fifteenth Chapter*. Ann Arbor (mimeographed copy of 1960 thesis).

Sollers, Philippe (1975), 'Joyce et Cie' in *Tel Quel,* no. 64, pp. 15–24.

Suter, August (1970), 'Some Reminiscences of James Joyce' in *James Joyce Quarterly,* vol. 7, no. 3, pp. 191–8.

Thornton, Weldon (1968), *Allusions in Ulysses,* North Carolina.


SECTION 3    MATERIAL NOT DIRECTLY RELATED TO JOYCE

Althusser, Louis (1965), *Pour Marx,* Paris. (Tr. *For Marx,* (London, 1969).)

Balzac, Honoré de (1963), *Œuvres complètes.* 40 vols in 21. Texte révisé et annoté par M. Bouteron et H. Longnon (Paris, 1926–63).

Barthes, Roland (1966), 'Introduction à l'analyse structurale des récits' in *Communications,* No. 8, pp. 1–27.

—— (1970), *S/Z* Paris.

—— (1973), *Le Plaisir du texte,* Paris.

—— (1977), *Image-Music-Text.* Essays selected and translated by Stephen Heath. London.

Benjamin, Walter (1973), *Illuminations,* edited and with an Introduction by Hannah Arendt. London.

—— (1973a), *Charles Baudelaire: A Lyric Poet in the Era of High Capitalism.* London.

—— (1973b), *Understanding Brecht.* Introduction by Stanley Mitchell. London.

Benveniste, Emile (1971), *Problems in General Linguistics.* Miami.

Bolton, Derek (1973), 'A Study towards an Understanding of the Philosophy of Wittgenstein.' Unpublished Ph.D. thesis. Cambridge.

Booth, Wayne (1961), *The Rhetoric of Fiction.* Chicago.

Boyle, J. W. (1961), 'The rise of the Irish Labour Movement, 1888–1907.' Unpublished Ph.D. thesis. Trinity College, Dublin.

Brecht, Bertolt and Eisler, Hans (1965), *The Measures Taken* in *The Jewish Wife and other short plays.* English versions by Eric Bentley. New York.

Brecht, Bertolt (1964), *Brecht on Theatre: the development of an aesthetic,* edited and translated by John Willett. London.

—— (1970a), *Sur le réalisme*. Texte français d'André Gisselbrecht. Paris.

—— (1970b), *Sur le cinéma*. Texte français de Jean-Louis Lebrave et de Jean-Pierre Lefebvre. Paris.

Burroughs, William S. (1974), *The Job*. Interviews with Daniel Odier. Revised edition with new introduction, 'Playback from Eden to Watergate' and 'Electronic Revolution 1970–71'. New York.

Cohn, Robert Greer (1949), *Mallarmé's Un Coup de Dès: an exegesis*. New Haven.

Derrida, Jacques (1967a), *De la grammatologie*. Paris.

—— (1967b), *L'Ecriture et la différence*. Paris.

—— (1972a), *La Dissémination*. Paris.

—— (1972b), *Marges* Paris.

—— (1972c), 'Entretien avec Derrida' in *La Quinzaine Littéraire* 16 to 30 novembre 1972, pp. 13–16.

Ducrot, O. (1968), 'Le structuralisme en linguistique' in *Qu'est-ce que le structuralisme?* edited by François Wahl. Paris.

Dummett, Michael (1959), 'Truth' in *Proceedings of the Aristotelian Society*, vol. 59, pp. 141–62.

Eisenstein, Sergei (1951), *Film Form: Essays in Film Theory*, edited and translated by Jay Leyda. London.

Eliot, George (1880), *The Works of George Eliot* (Cabinet edition), 20 vols. Edinburgh, 1878–1880.

Foucault, Michel (1967), 'Marx, Freud, Nietzsche' VIIᵉ Colloque Philosophique International de Royaumont, *Cahiers de Royaumont*, Philosophie, No. 6, pp. 183–92.

—— (1968), *L'Archéologie du savoir*. Paris.

Freud, Sigmund (1954), *The Origins of Psycho-Analysis*. Letters to Wilhelm Fliess, Drafts and Notes: 1887–1902, edited by Marie Bonaparte, Anna Freud, Ernst Kris. Authorised translation by Eric Mosbacher and James Strachey. Introduction by Ernst Kris. London.

——, *The Standard Edition of the Complete Psychological Works of Sigmund Freud*. Translated from the German under the general editorship of J. Strachey in collaboration with A. Freud, assisted by J. Strachey and A. Tyson. 23 vols, London,

1953–66. Volume 24. Indexes and bibliographies compiled by A. Richards. London 1974.

Greaves, Desmond C. (1972), *The Life and Times of James Connolly*. London.

Greimas, A. J. (1966), *Sémantique Structurale*. Paris.

Heath, Stephen, Colin MacCabe and Christopher Prendergast, (eds) (1971), *Signs of the Times: Introductory Readings in Textual Semiotics*. Cambridge.

Heath, Stephen (1972b), *The Nouveau Roman: A Study in the Practice of Writing*. London.

—— (1975), 'Film and System: Terms of Analysis.' Part 1, *Screen*, vol. 16, no. 1, pp. 7–77. Part 2, *Screen*, vol. 16, no. 2, pp. 91–113.

Hindess, Barry and Paul Hirst (1977), *Mode of Production and Social Formation: an auto-critique of Pre-Capitalist Modes of Production*. London.

Hjelmslev, Louis (1970), *Essais linguistiques*. Travaux du Cercle Linguistique de Copenhague, vol. XII, 2nd ed. Copenhagen.

Homer, *The Odyssey*, translated by E. V. Rieu. London, 1946.

Irigaray, Luce (1966), 'Communications linguistique et spéculaire' in *Cahiers pour l'Analyse*, no. 3, pp. 39–55.

Jolas, Eugene (1929), Manifesto, 'Revolution of the Word' in *transition*, nos. 16 and 17, p. 13.

Kristeva, Julia (1970), *Le Texte du roman: approche sémiologique d'une structure discursive transformationelle*. The Hague.

—— (1974), *La Révolution du langage poétique: l'avant-garde à la fin du XIXᵉ siècle: Lautréamont et Mallarmé*. Paris.

Lacan, Jacques (1966a), *Ecrits*. Paris.

—— (1966b), 'Réponses à des étudiants en philosophie sur l'objet de la psychanalyse.' Text edited by M. G. Contesse. *Cahiers pour l'Analyse*, no. 3, pp. 5–13.

—— (1973), *Le Séminaire. Livre XI. Les quatre concepts fondamentaux de la psychanalyse*. Paris.

—— (1975a), *Le Séminaire. Livre 1. Les écrits techniques de Freud*. Paris.

—— (1975b), *Le Séminaire. Livre XX. Encore*. Paris.

Laplanche, J. and Pontalis, J. B. (1973), *The Language of Psycho-*

*Analysis*. London.

Larmore, Charles (1975), 'Use and Representation in Wittgenstein.' Unpublished Paper.

Leavis, F. R. (1933b), 'Milton's Verse' in *Scrutiny*, vol. 2, no. 2, pp. 123–36.

Lenin, V. I., *Collected Works*. 45 vols. Translation of the fourth enlarged edition prepared by the Institute of Marxism-Leninism, Central Committee of the C.P.S.U., London, 1960–1970.

Lyons, F. S. L. (1973), *Ireland since the Famine*. London.

MacCabe, Colin (1974), 'Realism and the Cinema: Notes on some Brechtian theses' in *Screen*, vol. 15, no. 2, pp. 7–27.

—— (1975), 'The Politics of Separation' in *Screen*, vol. 16, no. 4, pp. 61–72.

—— (1977), 'Theory and Film: Principles of Realism and Pleasure' in *Screen*, vol. 17, no. 3, pp. 7–27.

Mallarmé, Stephane, *Oeuvres complètes*. Paris, 1945.

Mao Tse-tung, 'On Contradiction' in *Four Essays on Philosophy*. Peking, 1966, pp. 23–78.

Martinet, André (1973), *Eléments de linguistique générale*. Paris.

Marx, Karl and Engels, Friederich (1965), *The German Ideology*. London.

Marx, Karl, *The 18th Brumaire of Louis Bonaparte*. Moscow, 1972.

——, *Capital; a critical analysis of capitalist production*, 3 vols. London, 1974.

Miller, Jacques-Alain (1966), 'La Suture' in *Cahiers pour l'Analyse*, no. 1, pp. 37–49.

—— (1968), 'Action de la structure' in *Cahiers pour l'Analyse*, no. 9, pp. 93–105.

O'Casey, Sean (1919), *The Story of the Irish Citizen Army*, Dublin.

Pautrat, Bernard (1971), *Versions du soleil: Figures et système de Nietzsche*. Paris.

Plato, *The Symposium*. London, 1951.

Procacci, Giuliano (1973), *History of the Italian People*. London.

Propp, V. (1968), *Morphology of the Folktale*. First edition translated by Laurence Scott with an Introduction by Svatava

Pirkova-Jakobsen. 2nd edition revised and edited with a Preface by Louis A. Wagner. New Introduction by Alan Lundes. Austin.

Richards, I. A. and Ogden, C. K. (1923), *The Meaning of Meaning; a Study of the Influence of Language upon Thought and of the Science of Symbolism.* With an introduction by J. P. Postgate and supplementary essays by B. Malinowski and F. G. Crookshank. London.

Safouan, Moustafa (1968), 'De la structure en psychanalyse' in *Qu'est-ce que le structuralisme?* edited by François Wahl. Paris. pp. 239–98.

Saussure, Ferdinand de (1973), *Cours de linguistique générale.* Edition critique préparée par Tullio de Mauro. Paris.

Sollers, Philippe (1968), *Logiques.* Paris.

—— (1974), *Sur le matérialisme; De l'atomisme à la dialectique révolutionnaire.* Paris.

Stalin, J. *Collected Works,* vol. 1–13 (unfinished). Moscow 1952–55.

Tarski, Alfred (1949), 'The Semantic Conception of Truth' in *Readings in Philosophical Analysis,* edited by H. Feigl and W. Sellars. New York. pp. 52–84.

Terray, Emmanuel (1973), 'L'idée de Nation et les transformations du capitalisme' in *Les Temps Modernes,* nos 324–6, pp. 492–508.

Trubetskoy, N. S. (1969), *Principles of Phonology.* Berkeley and Los Angeles, 1969.

Wahl, François (1968), 'Philosophie et structuralisme' in *Qu'est-ce que le structuralisme?* Paris. pp. 301–442.

Waismann, Frederick (1967), *Wittgenstein und der Wiener Kreis.* Shorthand notes edited by B. F. McGuiness. Oxford.

Willemen, Paul (1974), 'The Fugitive Subject' in *Raoul Walsh,* edited by Phil Hardy, pp. 63–89.

Wittgenstein, Ludwig (1971), *Tractatus Logico-Philosophicus.* The German Text of Ludwig Wittgenstein's *Logisch-philosophische Abhandlung* with a new edition of the translation by D. F. Pears and B. F. McGuiness and with an Introduction by Bertrand Russell. London.

—— (1964), *The Blue and Brown Books*. Oxford.

—— (1967), *Philosophical Investigations*. Oxford.

—— (1974), *Philosophical Grammar,* edited by Rush Rhees. Oxford.

Yeats, W. B. (1904), *The Tables of the Law and The Adoration of the Magi*. London.

# Index

Entries for concepts refer to arguments in which the concepts figure and not to the occurrence of lexical items. Certain concepts, such as subject, discourse, narrative, occur throughout the text and therefore have not been included in the index.